Speaking, Listening and Understanding

Speaking, Listening and Understanding

English Language Debate for Non-Native Speakers

REVISED EDITION

Gary Rybold

Neill Harvey-Smith

International Debate Education Association

New York, London & Amsterdam

Published by:
International Debate Education Association
105 East 22nd Street
New York, NY 10010

Library of Congress Cataloging-in-Publication Data

Rybold, Gary.
  Speaking, listening and understanding : English language debate
for non-native speakers / Gary Rybold, Neill Harvey-Smith. --
Revised edition.
     pages cm
  ISBN 978-1-61770-081-1
  1. Debates and debating. 2. English language--Study and teach-
ing--Foreign speakers. I. Harvey-Smith, Neill. II. Title.
  PN4181.R94 2013
  808.53--dc23

                          2013027753

Design by Kathleen Hayes

Printed in the USA

 IDEBATE Press

Dedications

Gary Rybold:

> To Xiaoqing, whose love inspires me.

Neill Harvey-Smith:

> To Beth, Rosie, and James with all my love:
> the last debating book, I promise.

Contents

Preface

Speaking, Listening and Understanding is an introductory guide on how to debate. It is especially written for people who speak English as a second language.

Gary participated in his first debate in 1965. Neill made his first speech in 1996. Since then, we have met thousands of people who have found that the world of debate opened the doors of knowledge. At the heart of debate is a sharing of ideas and information. Ultimately, this book is about that sharing. We will share information that should help you get started in formal debating. Then, once you debate, you will share your ideas on a variety of topics. As you share, you will also learn new concepts, a new vocabulary, and a love for the exchange of ideas.

The aim of this book is to provide a simple debate text for new English language students, without the complexity or excessive cultural references that can make learning difficult. It was written with non-native English speakers in mind.

This guide identifies, explains, and teaches the skills common to all debating. The aim is to allow you to learn the basics. You can then apply them to whichever debate format you choose. Having taught English as a foreign language, we are convinced of the huge benefits that debating brings to language learning. If you are learning English, this book is written with you in mind.

Speaking, Listening and Understanding was written to make it easier for you to debate. Each chapter is short enough for you to read in one sitting. At the end of each chapter, you will find a list of the important concepts and key vocabulary terms used in that chapter. All definitions are listed in the Glossary at the end of the book. Each chapter teaches you a skill that the next chapter builds upon.

Chapter 1 welcomes you to debate and encourages you to be the best communicator that you can be. The skills you learn will help you think, speak, and learn in every language, including English.

Chapter 2 explains the basic concepts of debate. You will learn some of the rules and responsibilities of debate, how it works, and how to do it.

Chapter 3 discusses how to improve your speaking and performance skills, offering techniques for you to practice.

Chapter 4 demonstrates how to organize and structure a speech.

Chapter 5 describes some debate formats you might try, with different time limits, types of questions, and number of speakers.

Chapter 6 discusses propositions—how to move from a broad topic area to a clear and focused discussion.

Chapter 7 examines critical thinking. You will learn how to analyze arguments, compare viewpoints, and avoid thinking that is not logical.

Chapter 8 looks at research. It explains how to find evidence, use it effectively in the debate, and counter evidence provided by other teams.

Chapter 9 explains refutation. You will learn how to respond to arguments presented by other debaters and defend your own.

Chapter 10 describes tournaments and judging. You will get a sense of how a tournament works and the wonderful opportunities presented by competitive debate.

We would love for you to share your experiences in learning debate. If you read something in this book that is unclear or if you would like to see something added, please write to us. Please send all recommendations and comments through IDEA at www.idebate.org. We feel honored to be part of your learning experience and would appreciate your ideas. Good luck and good debating.

Gary Rybold

Neill Harvey-Smith

CHAPTER 1

Welcome to Debate

Speaking, Listening and Understanding covers a special kind of communication: debating. This chapter introduces the activity of debating and discusses the skills that you will gain if you participate in debates. Debating is a way to organize discussion of a topic. People make speeches for and against a statement called a *motion*. They argue against each other's points, trying to persuade judges or an audience that their arguments are the best. So, if you want to improve your listening and speaking skills, your presentation skills and your critical thinking abilities, read on! Debating is a great educational opportunity, but, above all, people debate because it is FUN.

Debating Teaches Skills

Public Speaking

Many people have a fear of public speaking. Did you know that speaking before an audience is the number one fear in the United States? Even ahead of snakes or dying? If the thought of standing up in front of a group and talking for seven minutes fills you with fear—don't worry. You are not alone. Yet, the thousands of debaters we have taught, coached, and judged have learned to love public speaking. Once they get over their fears, the excitement of competition kicks in, and the activity becomes more enjoyable with each debate. Debaters are developing skills that will help them for the rest of their lives. No wonder so many English teachers use debate as an effective and stimulating way to develop listening and speaking skills.

When you first started learning English, you may have begun with grammar rules. Often, students learn to read and write English before they practice their speaking skills. If this is your experience, speaking in English may not be as easy as writing in English. Actively finding the right words is harder than passive comprehension. You may feel that sharing ideas in a second language comes less easily. Debating will help you overcome these difficulties and develop your spoken English skills. Debating is like an immersion program: very soon, you will begin thinking in English. Not only that, but big competitions recognize the difficulty of debating in English as a Second Language (ESL) and reward the best ESL teams with separate finals, winners, and trophies.

Debates can help you to become a better speaker in all situations—private and public. Everyone in a debate contributes and has a voice. With new skills, you will be able to speak with greater confidence and power.

Of course, you will make mistakes. All debaters do. Debating uses the English language but it is not a test of your ability to speak grammatically perfect English. Non-native speakers can and do beat native speakers in debates. Debating rewards making arguments clearly, comprehensibly, and persuasively. As you practice thinking about your ideas and explaining them to others, you will gain confidence. As you gain confidence, you will express your ideas more clearly when you speak. Debating is something you must practice.

Debate also develops several other skills that will help you communicate effectively—in English or any other language.

Critical Thinking

Critical thinking is the discipline by which you ask better questions, evaluate answers, keep an open mind, are honest about your own biases, and make better decisions. You can improve several critical thinking skills by studying debate:

1. Debate will teach you how to develop good arguments and find the flaws in bad arguments. Arguments can be strong or weak. You will learn to construct and present the best arguments for your side and to understand

the strengths and weaknesses of your own and others' arguments.

2. Debate will teach you how to ask and answer insightful questions. When debaters learn to ask the right questions, they can determine the central points of an issue. When they respond to questions insightfully, they clarify their own thinking.

3. Debate will teach you how to solve problems. The purpose of the arguments you make, when taken together, is to find the best solution to a problem. You will learn how to make comparisons and determine the best solutions.

4. Debate will teach you how to use reliable sources of information. Not all information is good or useful. You will learn how to evaluate sources to find those that are most reliable and most valuable. You will gather evidence from many sources and assess and compare their arguments.

5. Debate will teach you to be aware of your personal and cultural biases. Arguing with diverse people from different cultures, traditions, and laws will force you to challenge your ideas of what is obvious, normal, or usual. Debating requires you to look deeply at questions and prove your assumptions.

Other Skills

1. *Researching*: Debate will help you become a better researcher. To be successful in debate, you need to understand both sides of an issue, support your position with relevant evidence, and handle evidence that strengthens your opponents' case. Using libraries and online materials to build your knowledge, you will learn how to evaluate material and organize it effectively.

2. *Writing*: Debate will help you become a better writer. Once you complete your research, you need to turn it into a speech by writing *briefs*, short arguments in note form that will help you articulate your point of view when you stand to speak.

3. *Listening*: Debate will help you become a better listener. When members of other teams are speaking, you must listen to what they say so that you can respond. You will also need to listen to your own partner if you are to advance your team's case.

4. *Note-taking*: debate will help you to become a better notetaker. Since debates may last an hour or more, you will need to write down what other teams say, what your partner says, and what you want to say. Because a debate is a live event, you will need to make notes quickly and legibly.

5. *Organizing*: Debate will help you to become a better organizer. Because each debate will involve many ideas, you must learn how to put them in and keep them in order—you must organize them. You want to make sure the audience understands your arguments and how they fit into the debate.

6. *Teamwork*: Debate will teach you teamwork because you must work and think as a team to succeed. You will have a partner and be assessed together on the case you make. You will need to share information, develop strategies, and communicate quickly. More broadly, you will need to take on knowledge and pick up skills from coaches and fellow students. Sometimes debate partners become friends for life. Even competing debaters from other schools can become the closest of friends.

Making the Most of Your Training

Debate can be one of the best educational experiences of your life. It can help with your English language skills. It can be exciting and fun. It can teach you skills that will last a lifetime. To make the most of your training, here are a few recommendations.

1. *Read any assignments before coming to class.* This book and any other materials will give you background before

a debate session. If you read and understand the material, the class will make more sense to you. Taking notes before a class enables you to come in seeking to apply your knowledge.

2. *Take notes in class.* Many cultures have the saying "in one ear and out the other." It means that what we hear, even if we are interested, we do not always remember. You should write down the main ideas the teacher presents along with your thoughts on these ideas. As you debate more, your note-taking skills will improve.

3. *Stay organized.* Be sure to organize your notes, so you can find what you have learned when you need it. Many debaters arrange what they have learned into a file and take it to their debates.

4. *Review the information.* After class, read your notes and think about what they mean. Write down any questions you have for the next class. Also, try explaining what you have learned to someone else. Teaching a new concept is a great way to learn.

5. *Ask questions.* As a debater, you must ask questions. If you do not understand a concept, do not be afraid to ask a teacher, coach, or experienced debater to explain it further.

6. *Practice.* This book and your coaches will give you many ideas about how to prepare for a debate. You will also have many opportunities to practice debating in groups. You learn most by doing. Take every chance to participate in debates. Practice asking and answering questions. Practice speeches and review them to see how you can improve in the future.

At the end of every debate, listen to what the judges, your coach, and other debaters have to say. This feedback lets you know what you are doing well and where you need to improve. Take notes on what they say. These comments are called *constructive criticism*—they are meant to improve your performance, not to make you feel bad about what you just did. Be sure to review them with your coach and teammates so you can improve.

To become a better debater and critical thinker, you need to read, listen, and speak. *Speaking, Listening and Understanding* is designed to explain what you need to know to get started in debate. It is a beginner's textbook. As you improve, you will want to read other books. I encourage you to continue your education after this course. Perhaps you will learn to love debate as we do and teach others.

Important Concepts in This Chapter

1. People debate for many reasons: to have fun, to take advantage of a great educational opportunity, and to learn effective English language skills.

2. Debate develops a variety of skills, including note-taking, organization, research, writing, listening, speaking, teamwork, and critical thinking.

3. To improve your chances of success in debate and in school, read assigned materials prior to class, take notes, stay organized, review information learned, ask questions, and practice.

4. However much you read and study, the best way to learn debating skills is to practice.

EXERCISES

1. Get a notebook just for debate. List and commit to the goals you hope to achieve by learning to debate.

2. Start a vocabulary list of new words that help you debate.

3. Read. Whether it is news, history, biography, philosophy, science, nothing develops the mind like reading.

KEY WORDS

brief	listening
coach	motion
constructive criticism	note-taking
critical thinking	organizing
English as a Second Language (ESL)	practice
judges	researching
	writing

CHAPTER 2

Debate Basics

This chapter outlines the basics of debating. You will learn who is involved in a debate, the purpose of a debate, and the responsibilities debaters have during a debate.

The fundamental feature of any debate is this: two sides agree to disagree about a specific topic, called the *motion*.

The Sides

A side can consist of one, two, three, four, or as many as six debaters, depending on the format you use. A side must either be for the topic or against the topic. When you debate, you call the other side your *opponents* (regardless of what side you are on). The sides can be called different things, depending on format and country, all of which will be understood:

For the topic	Against the topic
Government	Opposition
Proposition	Opposition
Affirmative	Negative
Pro	Con

To avoid confusion, in this book we use the Worlds Style terms *Government* and *Opposition* to label the sides for and against the motion.

In many formats, all the debaters on one side work as a single team, preparing together, planning their content together, and working together during the debate. However, in Worlds Style, each side of four is divided into two teams of two. Each team prepares and competes in isolation, discussing their content neither with the other side nor with the other team on their own side. In Worlds Style, the debaters sitting next to you may be on your side, but they are not on your team.

Usually, teams do not choose what side of the topic they defend. The sides are assigned at random. Because the speakers do not make that choice, teams do not need to believe in the side of the topic they support. Often, debaters find themselves arguing for ideas that they are privately against. In some debate activities, when the same topic is used for a whole season, debaters may switch sides. Whatever the case, you need to be able to think about an issue from all angles to become a good debater.

In preparation for a debate, teams often role-play to find the best arguments for their side in a process called *perspective taking* or *prep*, from the word *preparation*. Like a lawyer defending a guilty client, you may have to defend something that you don't believe. Perspective taking is a process of imagining yourself as holding lots of different viewpoints on the topic. It helps you keep an open mind while you search for the best arguments for the side you must defend.

Perspectives on Debate

Many debaters consider debate a game in which the participants sharpen their thinking and speaking skills. Like sports, debating has rules, teams, officials, winners, and losers. You can see it as mental and verbal gymnastics, with teams matching wits against each other. Your job, as a debater, is to find the path to victory.

Others think of debate as a laboratory where teams test their arguments against the arguments of another. Your job, in this approach, is to debate as well as you can, so the best arguments emerge. Certainly, debaters learn a great deal in the process of a debate that strengthens their ability to craft winning arguments in the future. As you improve as a debater, you become better at testing ideas and identifying their weak spots.

There is some truth in both these perspectives. Each allows debaters to focus on developing the best arguments for a position without relying solely on their personal beliefs. To remind everyone that debate is a contest of skills, not an exchange of heartfelt beliefs, debaters traditionally shake hands at the end of a debate.

Persuasion

The overall responsibility of a debater is to be *persuasive*. Being persuasive means putting across ideas in a way that will convince people who disagree to change their minds and strengthen the convictions of those who agree with you. A persuasive speech doesn't just make good points; it tells a story that gives an account of the whole debate. It shows how the two sides fit together and makes a compelling case that your version of events is the one that should prevail. And, it does all this with compelling delivery, a subject we consider in Chapter 3.

Burdens

A *burden* is a responsibility that a debater is given to fulfill. Judges evaluate debaters based on how persuasive they are. Thinking about how well a debater meets certain burdens is a useful model for setting expectations of a speech. Failure to meet these expectations is a weakness and may lead to a team losing the debate.

"Prove it!"—The Burden of Proof

There is a saying "those who assert must prove," and it is true in debating. Whoever wants to make a point (assertion) must provide reasoning and evidence (proof) that her point is right. Points are ideas that make up your case. When points are transformed into arguments by reasoning, they become the building blocks of a persuasive speech. Since neither debaters nor their audience are expected to be experts on the topic they are discussing, they must use evidence for each point they make. When a debater asserts a point without evidence, judges will not reward it. When credible reasoning is provided, points become golden and start to win you debates.

"Answer it!"—The Burden of Refutation

Refutation is the process of attacking arguments. If you present an argument in a debate and the other teams don't address it, insofar as the judges consider it to be a central, relevant point, they will give you great credit. Debate is not public speaking. You cannot just arrive with a speech and deliver it. You cannot simply guess how your ideas will be opposed and say a few lines that refute the points you expect to hear. Each team must debate the arguments actually made in the room. You should have something to say about the case every other team presents, even if it is to select just a couple of their arguments to refute. If you feel there is a common thread, you can group arguments together and respond to them with a single point. But you cannot ignore arguments made by other teams and expect to succeed. Remember, winning debates is about being persuasive. You must show the audience why the most convincing arguments of the other side are, on reflection, not as strong as they seem. To do that, you must engage meaningfully with the points other teams put forward.

"Analyze it!"—The Burden of Rejoinder

The saying for this burden is "answer the answer,"—sometimes called *clash*, like an imagined sword fight. A good debate is like a good table tennis match: when one team hits the ball, the other team returns it. The other team *refutes* what you say. But it doesn't stop there. You have to then defend your point and show what their analysis has missed. You may then get into a long rally of ideas. This back-and-forth arguing over a few central points is something at which the best debaters excel. Debaters often instinctively want to *go wider*, to show breadth, to make as many different arguments as they can, and see which ones stick in the imagination of the judges. But the best debaters *go deeper*, finding layers of analysis and closely examining alternatives raised by other teams in the room.

Roles

The first speech in a debate is very different from the last. The initial speaker needs to set out the parameters of the discussion, introduce central arguments, and lay the foundations of the debate before other teams get up and take shots at it. The final speaker may have already heard almost an hour of material from other speakers and will need to engage with the best of it with lots of refutation and clash. These are different types of speech. Imagine if the initial speaker tried to spend all his time refuting—what would he refute? Or a final speaker who ignored the rest of the debate and presented her own new arguments, trying to take the discussion in a totally new direction—how confusing would that be?

Debate has many formats and each has its own expectations, but all of them assign value to how well a speaker performs his role in the debate. Learn what your format demands, and shape your speech around the role you need to perform to make the debate work.

Note-Taking

Debate is a live and spontaneous activity, not an opportunity to read out speeches. Therefore, taking notes is an important skill. Ideally, your notes should be the shortest they possibly can be while still following what is happening in the debate. There are different ways to organize notes during a debate. You can write down each point and connect all things people say about it. You can draw a box for each speaker and note what they say. When you speak, it is important that you are not lost in your notes or tied to them. They should simply help you to remember. Personalized abbreviations can be a neat way to make the job easier. Using ? for a bad point, ! for a good one, [ ] for your thoughts on the point, R for rebuttal—it doesn't matter how you do it, as long as you understand it and it works for you.

The Decision

Debates have one or more judges who decide the winners and losers. Judges must apply the rules. They give the win to the team that they consider did the best job in that debate. They are not allowed to consider a team's previous record or vote for the side of the topic that they personally support.

In tournaments, judges fill out a written ballot with the result and the scores they gave to each speaker. These are used to help the tournament director assign the right teams to the right debates in the next round.

The judges must also justify their decisions to the debaters. In many formats, this is done in an *oral adjudication*: judges tell the teams what they thought about the debate and why the teams were placed in the order they were. This is a great opportunity for debaters to learn about what they did well and identify areas for improvement.

Important Concepts in This Chapter

1. Debates take place between two teams, with at least one debater on each team. Teams are either for an issue (Government) or against the same issue (Opposition).

2. There are different perspectives on debate: we can see it as a game, a sport, a laboratory for testing ideas. What all these perspectives have in common is acknowledging that debate is about persuasion—moving and shaping the views of others.

3. Debaters must persuade judges. They need to meet three burdens: burden of proof (prove it!), burden of refutation (answer it!), and burden of rejoinder (analyze it!).

4. Debaters each have a specific role in the debate, which varies from format to format. Understanding your role is vital to crafting your speech.

5. Note-taking is a good way for each speaker to follow what is happening in the debate so she can refer to the notes in her own speech.

6. Judges decide who won the debate based on which team did the best job of debating, not on whether they agree with the arguments presented. They offer reasons for choosing the winning team to help you improve.

EXERCISES

1. Choose a motion and write out three arguments in favor. Say your arguments aloud, using reasoning and evidence for each point. Then think of three responses to

your arguments. Say them aloud. Return to your original points and defend them. Then attack them again! Do it for as long as you can continue to improve the depth of your arguments.

KEY WORDS

---

argument	perspective taking
assertion	persuasive
burden	point
clash	prep
grouping	proof
motion	refutation
note-taking	rejoinder
opponent	role
oral adjudication	side

CHAPTER 3

Delivery for Effective Speaking

This chapter discusses how best to prepare yourself mentally and physically for a debate. Debating can make you nervous because you are speaking in public on a subject about which you may know little and presenting ideas that your opponent will attack. That's a lot to prepare for! Becoming a more confident speaker will help you in your debating. The manner in which you speak is a big part of what makes you persuasive and wins you debates.

When learning to debate, you are also learning how to become a better speaker. As the delivery of your speeches becomes smoother, you should become more confident—not only with your English language skills but also with your critical thinking and analytical skills. The skills we review in this and the next chapter will help in any communication scenario—whether you are having an informal conversation or speaking to a large audience.

Fighting Your Fears

Sometimes people have good ideas but are so nervous, uncertain, quiet, or boring in their presentation that the audience does not fully listen to them or believe their words. I also know people who can take the weakest ideas and sell them brilliantly to an audience with great delivery. Your goal is to be the best of and in both worlds. A brilliant speaker takes good ideas, adds great reasoning, and puts them across as genuine, with enthusiasm and energy. An honest person genuinely involved in what he is saying is like a magnet to any audience.

First, let's talk about nervousness. Many people have a fear of public speaking. So, don't worry if you feel nervous. Anxiety is your body's way of preparing you for a dangerous situation. Think about how our ancestors had to protect themselves from wild animals—fighting or running away. To survive, they needed a good *fight or flight* response. Your brain thinks public speaking is a dangerous situation, so your body finds a way to increase your strength. Your heart may beat faster, sending oxygen around your body, making you red in the face and agitated. You find it hard to catch your breath as you talk. Your hands and feet may start moving in ways you don't readily control. All of this comes from the extra energy your body is producing.

The trick is to use this extra energy to your advantage. Nerves, used the right way, can help your delivery.

Preparation, practice, and performance can all help you achieve your goals.

Preparing Yourself for Public Speaking

Practice Deep Breathing

Regulating your breathing can help to deal with anxiety. Close your eyes, think of a pleasant place or a positive memory, and a do a minute or two of slow breathing—in through your nose, out through your mouth. Just a few deep breaths can help.

Drink Plenty of Water

If you are nervous, a common result is a dry throat or cough. Have water available and sip it when you need it.

Have a Positive Attitude

Your attitude should be: "I can do this. I am a smart person. I am learning a new skill. This is exciting." Millions of others have stood in your shoes, speaking in public for the first time. They have learned and so will you. Remember positive experiences in your life, especially those involving performance, like acting or telling a joke that people enjoyed. Think back to them and remember how it felt—all the fun, the positive energy around. When remembering, try to tap into that feeling and use it when you stand up to speak. If you set a confident tone, people will pick up on it.

Use High Energy

I don't mean wave your hands around. Nerves are normal and they make you feel energetic. Use that energy in a positive way—to make your posture straight and strong, your voice louder and more resonant, your intonation clearer, your face expressive, your hands joining in with your words. There is a well-established perception gap between how energetic we feel our performance is and how energetic others perceive it to be. You may feel highly animated but others may see you as flat. Err on the side of high energy. Be slightly louder, more expressive, and more passionate than you think you need to be. Do it consistently and you will hit the spot that inspires people.

Offer No Disclaimers

A *disclaimer* is when you deny responsibility for something. Some people use a disclaimer before they speak, like "I am very nervous, so this won't be very good" or "you must excuse me, I don't know anything about this topic." This only prepares the audience for a bad performance. Sometimes people indulge in disclaimers in other ways, giving away the part of their speech they feel is weakest by speaking more quietly, talking faster, or having more reserved body language like folded arms. Your words, your voice, your body should emphasize the message: "This is a good speech. I feel confident giving it."

Concentrate on the Audience

The audience came to hear you. They are open to persuasion. The other teams are going to disagree with you. That is their job. If you look at the people opposite pulling pained faces, shaking their heads, asking you skeptical questions, and take your cue from them, you will be too defensive, too quiet, too beaten down with negativity to reach levels that can inspire the audience.

Breathe

A speech should delight the audience. To achieve brilliance in performance, you cannot talk at 100 miles per hour. Leave pauses after major points to emphasize their importance and let them settle into the minds of the audience. Breathe to allow your voice to maintain its strength throughout your speech. Breathing achieves so much—making the body relax, the voice strengthen, the natural cadence of speech sing through your words. Treat it as an essential skill of speechmaking.

Practice

Although preparing your body and mind is very important, practice is the key to reducing your speech anxiety and winning debates. How should you practice?

Out Loud

Speeches don't live on paper. They live in your voice and the ears and imaginations of the audience. So practice them aloud. As you hear the words, you will understand where you need to clarify your points or present them in a more exciting way. As you say the words, you will learn which phrases or arguments make the most impact.

With Your Notes

Use the notes and notation style you really use in a competitive debate. It is no good writing out neat longhand if in real debates you only have time for scruffy shorthand.

Make sure you get used to translating what is on the page into what has been and is to be said.

In Front of an Audience

Use family, friends, coaches, other debaters, anyone who will volunteer. If you can't find an audience or want to see how you look, practice in front of the mirror. It was good enough for Winston Churchill, so it is good enough for you!

Using the Delivery Techniques

You will read about standing and speaking, breathing, gesturing, and eye contact below. Follow all of the delivery guidelines during your practice sessions.

After Each Tournament

If you lose a debate you shouldn't have lost or an argument didn't come across as you planned because of the way you described it, practice it when you get home. Study your notes and the judge's feedback. Consider ways you can improve your speech. Consolidate all the comments and rework your case. You never know when it may come up again.

New Words Make Your Point Stronger

If English is not your first language, it can be tough to find the right word at the right moment. Consider the vocabulary everyone used in the debate, look up any unfamiliar words, and review the language you used. Remember, the best words are not the longest words, just the simplest words that make your point.

Delivery

Now that you understand how to control your nerves, you need to learn the elements of good delivery to make your speeches sound better and make you look better delivering them.

Be Yourself

You don't have to become an actor or swallow a dictionary. Just be you. Speak as if you are having a conversation about something that you care deeply about. Be you when you are at your most confident and passionate. Be genuine. Be enthusiastic.

Use Vocal Variety

If you speak in a monotone—where everything is at the same pitch—a listener finds her brain switching off and is lulled to sleep. Instead, allow your thoughts and emotions to come to life by the way you say your words. Vary your tone of voice and speed of delivery to help bring out your meaning. If you say "this is one of the biggest challenges facing our planet" but sound like a bored robot, your audience won't feel that you are genuine, enthusiastic, and passionate. Emphasize important words with a stress. After an important sentence, pause. When making a new point, speak louder so people get that it is a headline. Be sure to pronounce your words properly and clearly. If that means slowing down, slow down!

Speak Up

Make sure that everyone in the room can hear you. Because non-native speakers of English can feel uncertain of their words, they can sometimes whisper or mumble to cover any possible mistakes. Debaters should project their voices to the back of the room. Projecting shows confidence and keeps the audience engaged. This is much more important than hiding grammatical errors.

Control Your Body

When energy is flowing through your body, it can come out in negative ways that hurt your delivery. The best way to control your body is to practice using a relaxed, strong position from which to deliver your speeches. Remember the following:

- *Plant your feet.* Have a strong base position with your feet planted flat on the floor, below and parallel with your shoulders. Good presenters do not walk aimlessly around the room or nervously move their legs or feet as they speak. Movement should be *motivated*—that is, it should have a purpose. If you step closer to the audience to make an emotional appeal, then back to your notes for the next point, that may be effective. But circling the podium out of pure nervous energy just distracts the audience.

- *Relax your arms.* To gesture, you need a base position from which your arms and hands can join in. You can keep them loose by your side. You can keep them in front of your stomach, one hand in a loose fist cupped by the other hand. What matters is that they can easily join in with your speech. Repetitive gestures or waving are a distraction. Gestures also should be *motivated*—they should fit the content being spoken. If you have a lectern, you can rest your hands on the top but don't grab or lean on it—it will make you tense and tie you to that spot. Leave your hands free to gesture and communicate.

- *Make eye contact with the audience.* Look different audience members in the eye. Try telling a member of the audience a complete thought before going to the next member. In a big room, make sure you speak to all four corners. Vary your eye contact and see what works for you. Always focus on the audience, even when other teams are asking you questions. It is the audience and judges whom you are trying to convince.

- *Don't play with your notes.* If you keep notes, place them on the lectern or table and refer to them as little as possible. Good debaters make a speech feel natural and spontaneous. Speeches should never be read out.

- *If you have a microphone, test it before you start your speech.* Once it is in the right place, don't touch it. Always leave at least six inches between your mouth and the microphone.

Important Concepts in This Chapter

1. Developing confidence greatly improves your speaking skills.

2. Improving your public speaking skills involves fighting your fears, preparation, practice, and focusing on delivery.

3. Practice is the key to success.

EXERCISES

1. Go to the library and get a short story or use a nursery rhyme you remember from childhood. Read the story out loud so that the words come to life. Stand up and tell the story using appropriate gestures to bring it to life. Ideally, find yourself an audience of family or friends so you can practice storytelling with eye contact. It will feel strange at first, but it is a good way to practice focusing energy.

2. Find a news article and read it out loud for effectiveness. Put the text down on the table and summarize the article to others using vocal variety and gestures. Be passionate. Deliver it like you are delivering a speech to a large audience.

KEY WORDS

arms	microphone
audience	monotone
breathe	motivation
delivery	nerves
disclaimer	notes
energy	pause
eye contact	practice
fight or flight	public speaking
legs	vocal variety

CHAPTER 4

Organization for Debating

There is no single ideal way to organize a speech. Every individual personality, issue, and progression of ideas will throw together a unique contribution for that speaker on that day. But a disorganized speech will never be ideal. Method is required to piece together the parts of a great speech. Done brilliantly, nobody will see the seams or notice the craftsmanship.

The key principle is to present your ideas in a way that enables the audience to follow your speech easily. Debates involve many arguments. If the judges do not know where your ideas fit into the debate, they may not appreciate their strengths. There is more to making great speeches, but this is the basic requirement. Let us explore one possible structure for a speech.

1. Grabber
2. Case Statement
3. Preview
4. Body
5. Summary
6. Conclusion

Grabber

The goal of the grabber is to get the attention of the audience. The grabber is designed to get people to stop and truly listen to you, to feel "this is going to be good."

A good introduction can give you confidence and help you win the acceptance of the audience. The first part of the speech sets the standard for the rest. If you are nervous and begin quietly and hesitantly, it will be easy to settle into a nervous and hesitant pattern. If you are confident, you raise the judges' expectations in a positive way, establishing credibility quickly.

A grabber can take many forms. Here are just a few:

a. An example. A (very brief) story of a person or people profoundly affected by the topic under discussion can help to set the tone for the importance, scale, and consequences your speech will detail.

b. A statistic. A killer statistic you intend to rely upon, if it is genuinely surprising, can be a grabber to help the audience understand the importance, scale, and consequences that your speech will bring out.

c. A joke. If you are good at telling jokes, and the joke sets the right tone for your speech, it is a great way to get people on your side and feeling positive about you.

d. A piece of refutation. If there is one single moment in your opponent's speech on which everything turns—the moment you go from full-throated agreement to outright opposition—then it can be dramatic to point that out, without any context, as a way to grab attention for everything to follow.

What matters is to get people's attention immediately and make them feel positive about you and your speech.

Case Statement

So, you have their attention. What next? The story. Before you launch into your arguments, the judges and audience need some sense of narrative. We call this narrative or story the *case*. Your case is the story of the debate as your team sees it: what your opponents say, what you say, and why, on balance, you are right. To work out your case, think about whether you disagree on only the *policy* being discussed or also on the *problem* it is supposed to address. Here is an example of how this section might sound: "The Government tells you that diamond smuggling is a grave and urgent problem, fueling misery and war. We agree. But they then claim that banning the purchase of diamonds will be an effective remedy. That is where we disagree." Judges find this kind of opening really useful. The debater is making clear where the two sides clash.

Preview

Having drawn dividing lines, you need to show how your speech will further your case. You can do this with a one-line preview of each of the main points you personally will make. If you like, you can number them. This is called *signposting*. Try to avoid being too general in your one-line previews. Compare and contrast:

> "First, I will talk about the problem. Second, I will discuss the causes of the problem. Third, I will tell you about the solutions to this problem."

> "First, I will tell you why the diamond trade is wrong. Second, I will discuss the role of organized criminal and paramilitary gangs in causing the problem. Third, I will tell you why a ban on diamond purchases is a key step toward solving the problem."

Note how much richer and more interesting is the second example. We haven't made the arguments yet, but the judges and audience know what is coming and can follow the narrative arc.

Body

The body of your speech is the combination of refutation and arguments you make to further your case. It is where you provide all of the arguments that prove your thesis. In terms of time, the body would normally constitute 75–90 percent of the total speech. When you organize your ideas, use a pattern that enables the audience to follow easily the progress of your arguments. If you have set out a good Case Statement and Preview, they will recognize the pattern when it comes.

Other chapters help you to create excellent refutation and arguments. Here, let us focus on how to organize them. The goal is to integrate various points into a system that enables you to make sense of a debate. A tried and tested method for persuasive speeches is to group them into the different types of argument: Principles, Practicalities, and Consequences.

a. Principles are arguments about whether something is right in the abstract. The question is whether we should do something according to an accepted framework of moral principles. Do people have the right to buy anything they want? Should they have that right? Is it ever right for governments to restrict markets? Under what circumstances? Note that these are not questions that can be resolved empirically, by taking evidence from the world and looking at it, but need to be explored on an ethical level. All debates involve some discussion of principles, so your team *must* have something to say about them.

b. Practicalities are arguments about whether a plan will work. The question is whether we can do the thing we are setting out to do. Would a ban on diamond purchases work or would people buy them on the black market? If we are discussing taking military action against a country to change its policies or structure, would the action result in the change or changes we desire? These are questions requiring detailed analysis of how policy or structures get transformed in the real world. All debates that propose a course of action are open to practical arguments.

c. Consequences are arguments about the effects of a plan once implemented. The question is whether, on balance, we will secure more benefits than incur costs by putting the plan into place. Think of all the different people and groups affected by a policy. Think of long-term as well as immediate effects. Think of the precedents it may set for action in other related areas. Any proposition that suggests making a change in the world always has many varied and interesting potential consequences.

Summary

Once the body of your speech is delivered, summarize the points you have made. Repeating your points will help your judges and audience to remember them. You can also remind them how the points you have made further the case you outlined at the start. This reinforcement makes everything feel like it fits together, every point seem like it has a broader purpose.

Conclusion

Just as you hooked people with your grabber, you want to send them away happy with a brilliant conclusion. You might use one of the same techniques—a story, statistic, or joke. You might also set a challenge to your opponents—what you believe they must say or do to convince a fair-minded person to change her position. They may duck the challenge, or even succeed, but, in drawing clear dividing lines for the judges, you will have achieved something valuable and important.

In debating, you do not write a speech from beginning to end. Rather, debate requires spontaneous responses as the dynamics change and new, unexpected points emerge. This uncertainty makes good organization very important—to ensure that your speech has a shape. Whatever happens, knowing that you need to find certain elements, in a certain order, can help you delay committing to certain points until the last possible moment. This will bring a freshness and vigor to your speeches that will help you win debates.

Organization is central to good debating. It will give you more confidence, help the audience understand you, and, consequently, you will have a better chance of meeting the goal of your speech.

Important Concepts in This Chapter

1. The key principle of organizing a speech is to present your ideas in a way that makes them easy to follow.

2. One way to organize a speech is: grabber, case summary, preview, body, summary, and conclusion.

3. The grabber gets the attention of the audience.

4. The case statement tells the story of the debate as your team sees it.

5. The preview shows how your speech will further your case.

6. The body is a combination of arguments and refutation. Three types of arguments you should look out for: principles, practicalities, and consequences.

7. The summary is a reminder of your speech and how it furthered your case.

8. The conclusion is a short, dramatic closing that sends the judges and audience away feeling good.

9. Organization is central to good debating.

EXERCISES

1. Find a newspaper article that makes a case. Using the model of organization in this chapter, rearrange and argue the main points of the article in your own words, following the structure.

2. Go over notes from previous debates. Try to add grabbers and conclusions that would have given them a bigger impact.

KEY WORDS

---

arguments	consequences
benefits	costs
body	ethical
case	grabber
conclusion	narrative

---

policy

practicalities

preview

principles

problem

rebuttal

signposting

statistics

summary

CHAPTER 5

Debate Formats

To ensure that everyone has a fair chance to speak, debates have specific rules about speaking order and time limits for each speech. These rules vary depending on the debate format. This chapter discusses the general format of a debate and presents an overview of five popular debate formats.

One of the great things about debate is that everyone is assured of an equal opportunity to speak. During your speaking time, you can express your ideas about the topic and what the other teams have said about the topic. In arguments that you have outside of debate, this may not be true. Some people may speak more than you or interrupt you. Some may get angry and raise their voices, talk over you, or even threaten you! This should never happen in a debate. Debate allows for a fair exchange in which all debaters know how much time they have and when they will speak. It is governed by rules that everyone agrees to follow. The arrangement of the rules is called a *debate format*.

Debate offers many different formats with various numbers of participants and time limits. In classroom debates, the teacher may decide to experiment with new rules to fit time schedules or to allow everyone to participate. You might start with one-minute speeches or allow everyone to make floor speeches after the main contributions to the debate. Regardless of the format, everyone should get to participate and debaters and judges should be made aware of the rules.

General Debate Format

Debates have two sides: the Government, which supports the motion, and the Opposition, which rejects the motion. The Government usually begins the debate, arguing for a change. The Opposition then knows exactly what they are speaking against. Both sides have an equal amount of speaking time. A judge usually keeps time for the speeches, knocking the table or ringing a bell to tell speakers when their time is up.

Five Popular Debate Formats

The remainder of this chapter sets out five of the most popular debate formats. You may choose to try them out in your own practice. They are Worlds Style, NPDA, Lincoln-Douglas, Policy Debate, and Karl Popper.

Worlds Style

Worlds Style is sometimes known as British Parliamentary. It is the format used in the World University Debating Championships. In Worlds Style, four teams compete at the same time, with two two-person teams on the Government and two two-person teams on the Opposition. All speeches are seven minutes long. The four teams prepare their arguments separately and all compete against one another. The judges rank the teams from first to fourth based on persuasiveness—the strength of their arguments combined with the manner of their delivery.

Debaters are rewarded for a combination of *matter*, which should be relevant, logical, and consistent, and *manner*, which comprises style and structure. Because teams are marked separately, it is possible for one Government team to come in first, while the other comes in fourth. Performing your role in the debate is especially important in Worlds Style. Worlds Style also recognizes the importance of overcoming the language barrier in debate, with special English as a Second Language (ESL) finals, winners, and awards at major championships.

Except for the first and last minute of each speech, debaters on the other side can ask *points of information*. These are questions or statements designed to challenge, highlight inconsistencies, or introduce a line of argument the speaker wants to pursue. A point of information can be rejected by saying "No, thank you," or accepted, in which case it must be answered.

The speaking order and time limits are as follows:

Announcement of topic and preparation time	15 minutes
Prime Minister (Opening Government)	7 minutes
Leader of the Opposition (Opening Opposition)	7 minutes
Deputy Prime Minister (Opening Government)	7 minutes
Deputy Leader of the Opposition (Opening Opposition)	7 minutes
Member of the Government (Closing Government)	7 minutes
Member of the Opposition (Closing Opposition)	7 minutes
Government Whip (Closing Government)	7 minutes

Opposition Whip (Closing Opposition)	7 minutes

National Parliamentary Debate Association (NPDA)

NPDA requires a different motion for every round. The assembly participant introduces it just like a member might in a national legislature. You might debate motions such as: "The government should take more action to reduce water pollution."

Tournaments usually have six rounds. In each round, the tournament host will assign teams to debate on the *Government* or *Opposition* side of a new topic. Once the topic is announced, the teams have 15 minutes preparation time before the opening speech is delivered. In debate competitions, each two-person team will debate three times on the government side and three times on the opposition side.

The first four speeches are constructive speeches during which the debaters may present new arguments. The first propositional speaker is called the *Prime Minister* (PM). The first oppositional speaker is called the *Leader of the Opposition* (LO). The next speaker is the *Member of the Government* (MG). Finally, the *Member of the Opposition* (MO) speaks.

The last two speeches are rebuttal speeches, during which the debaters can present no new arguments. The LO has the first rebuttal speech and the PM finishes the debate. There are no cross-examination periods in parliamentary debate, but the other team may ask for a *point of information* of the speaker during the constructive speeches. The other team uses points of information to ask a question to clarify or make a point. You do this by standing up during an opponent's constructive speech and asking "Point of information?" The speaker does not have to take the question and may say "Not at this time." If the speaker takes a question, he must answer it. No questions can be asked during the rebuttal speeches or during the first minute or last minute of each constructive speech.

Because no new arguments are allowed in the rebuttals, the other team may interrupt the speaker with a *point of order* to ask the judge to determine if the speaker is presenting a new argument. To do so, a debater stands and says, "Point of order." The judge then says, "State your point." The debater must then explain why she thinks the argument is new. The judge may decide it is not new and allow the argument to stay in the round. The judge would then say, "Point not well taken." If the judge agrees that it is a new argument and he will not consider the argument in the debate, he will say "Point well taken." The judge may also say, "Taken under consideration" and decide later if the argument was new or not.

The speaking order and time limits are:

Announce topic and preparation time	15 minutes

Constructive Speeches

Prime Minister Constructive (PMC)	7 minutes
Leader of the Opposition Constructive (LOC)	8 minutes
Member of the Government Constructive (MGC)	8 minutes
Member of the Opposition Constructive (MOC)	8 minutes

Rebuttal Speeches

Leader of the Opposition Rebuttal (LOR)	4 minutes
Prime Minister Rebuttal (PMR)	5 minutes

Note: There is no additional preparation time between speeches, just the 15 minutes given before the debate begins.

Lincoln-Douglas

Lincoln-Douglas is inspired by the debates between Abraham Lincoln and Stephen Douglas back in 1858. It involves two people: one for the affirmative and one for the negative. Lincoln-Douglas debate sometimes uses the **same topic throughout the year**. College debates use a policy topic, while high schools debate a value topic (such as whether or not globalization does more harm than good). The main differences between Lincoln-Douglas and team debate are that there are fewer speeches and you cannot depend on a partner to help you.

Note that even though the same kinds of speech are not the same length for each side, both teams have the same total speaking time. The speaking order and time limits are:

First Affirmative Speech	8 minutes
Cross-Examination	3 minutes
First Negative Speech	12 minutes
Cross-Examination	3 minutes
Second Affirmative Speech	6 minutes
Second Negative Speech	6 minutes
Third Affirmative Speech	4 minutes

Preparation Time: Each debater is allowed six minutes preparation time for the entire debate.

Policy Debate

Policy Debate has existed in the United States for more than 100 years. Typically, policy debaters address the same topic for the entire school year and regularly read evidence word-for-word during the debate to support their arguments. The topic is framed as a policy, for example: "There should be a change in the way Organization X does Y."

Policy Debate calls for two teams: the affirmative and the negative. The first four speeches are each nine minutes long, and each is called a constructive speech. During these speeches, debaters may propose or advance new arguments. After each constructive speech, the other team is allowed to cross-examine for no longer than three minutes. The affirmative gives the first constructive speech, followed by a cross-examination from the negative team. The negative gives the second constructive speech, followed by a cross-examination from the affirmative team. The affirmative is allowed to speak again for the third constructive speech, after which it is again cross-examined by the negative. Finally, the negative gives the fourth and final constructive speech, after which the affirmative cross-examines the negative. The teams use all four of their constructive speeches to propose their arguments and inform the audience about their evidence and give their reasoning in support of their arguments.

The last four speeches of the debate are called *rebuttals*. During a rebuttal speech, the debaters are not allowed to present new arguments, just challenge the arguments the other team introduced in its constructive speeches. Debaters also use rebuttal speeches to defend their team's arguments from challenges by the other team. Each rebuttal lasts six minutes. The negative gives the first rebuttal speech. The affirmative gives the second. The negative is allowed to speak again for the third, and the affirmative gives the fourth and final rebuttal speeches.

The speaking order and time limits are as follows:

Constructive speeches

First Affirmative Constructive (1AC)	9 minutes
Cross-Examination (of 1AC by 2NC)	3 minutes
First Negative Constructive (1NC)	9 minutes
Cross-Examination (of 1NC by 1AC)	3 minutes
Second Affirmative Constructive (2AC)	9 minutes
Cross-Examination (of 2AC by 1NC)	3 minutes
Second Negative Constructive (2NC)	9 minutes

Cross-Examination (of 2NC by 2AC)	3 minutes

Rebuttal speeches

First Negative Rebuttal (1NR)	6 minutes
First Affirmative Rebuttal (1AR)	6 minutes
Second Negative Rebuttal (2NR)	6 minutes
Second Affirmative Rebuttal (2AR)	6 minutes

Preparation Time: Because the debates are complex, long, and require significant evidence, each team is allowed a total of 10 minutes to prepare its speeches. Thus, if a team takes two minutes preparation time before its first speech, the team then has eight minutes remaining for preparation before their other speeches to apportion as they wish.

Karl Popper

The Karl Popper debate format calls for two teams: affirmative and negative. Each team has three debaters, with each debater speaking once in the debate. The same topic can be debated for the whole year or the topics can be new for each tournament.

The speaking order and time limits are as follows:

Affirmative Constructive	6 minutes
First Negative Cross-Examination	3 minutes
Negative Constructive	6 minutes
First Affirmative Cross-Examination	3 minutes
First Affirmative Rebuttal	5 minutes
Second Negative Cross-Examination	3 minutes
First Negative Rebuttal	5 minutes
Second Affirmative Cross-Examination	3 minutes
Second Affirmative Rebuttal	5 minutes
Second Negative Rebuttal	5 minutes

Preparation Time: Each team is allowed a total of eight minutes of preparation between speeches.

Karl Popper permits three students on a team, each speaking once. Its combination of separate constructive speeches, rebuttal speeches, and cross-examination distinguish it from formats like Worlds Style, where all the content must be covered in a single speech and complemented with points of information.

Conclusion

The formats have in common a goal of making each debate as fair as possible. Like any sport, debate has rules that allow the competitors to prepare and give all the competitors an equal chance to win. You can easily use the formats we have discussed or create your own. Fairness is the number one goal when setting up a debate.

Important Concepts in This Chapter

1. Debate formats include Worlds Style, NPDA, Lincoln-Douglas, Policy debate, and Karl Popper debate, and many more.

2. All formats have a Government and Opposition team, sometimes known by other names, both of which have the same amount of total speaking time.

EXERCISES

1. Try debating in different formats and notice the differences between them.

2. Have a go at points of information and cross-examination—you may learn valuable skills that you can use in your own favorite format.

KEY WORDS

affirmative	Opposition
British Parliamentary	Parliament
con	point of information
constructive speech	point of order
Government	point not well taken
Karl Popper	point well taken
leader of the opposition	Policy Debate
Lincoln-Douglas	prime minister
member	pro
negative	rebuttal
NPDA	state your point

CHAPTER 6

Propositions

The two sides in a debate need a specific subject area or *topic* to argue over. This topic is worded in the form of a *motion*—a question or statement to be argued. Then the Government must turn the motion into a *proposition*—a specific course of action. This chapter teaches you how to develop an effective proposition.

Let's start with a motion. It might take the form of a statement like "development aid should be conditional on improvements in human rights protections." In Worlds Style, you add, "This House Believes . . ." or "This House Would Make . . ." reflecting the traditions of Parliamentary debate from which it grew. When setting a motion, you must consider the following:

- The motion must be debatable. People must be able to disagree. For example, you couldn't debate the topic "humans need oxygen to live" since it is plainly true.

- The motion should be as simple as it can be to create the debate intended. The motion "all online information should be free and available to everyone" requires teams to prove a) that information should be free and b) that information should be available to everyone. If you mean "freely available" or just "available," take out the words you don't need. The simplest topics can lead to the richest debates.

- The motion should inspire enough arguments on both sides to give all teams a chance. Purely moral questions like "is it wrong to give aid to countries with a space program?" tend not to generate the material needed to last through an hour or more of debate. Make sure the motion has a practical angle and many potential consequences over which debaters can scrap.

Propositions

Propositions of Value

A proposition of value requires debaters to persuade the judges and audience to accept or reject an opinion. In Worlds Style, it is known as an *analysis debate*. Rather than persuading a Parliament that a course of action should be begun, the aim is to provide evidence for one subjective opinion about a topic over another subjective opinion. "Is

Iraq better off because of the 2003 invasion?" is an example of an analysis debate. Speakers need to argue about the criteria by which to judge if the country is "better off," as well as disputing how far the facts fit those criteria. When you argue a proposition of value, you are trying to provide evidence that your subjective opinion is better, by some disputable standard, than the other team's.

Arguing a proposition of value involves more steps than making a statement and backing it up with a measurement. You need to provide a specific definition of the value term you are discussing. "Better off" may break down to economic well-being, deaths by violence, human rights protection, democratic elections, all of these, and more. The term *better off* is not a fact; it is an opinion, since some people will report feeling worse off despite having the right to vote, others will feel better off in the teeth of oppression. Unless you set specific criteria, no meaningful debate can occur. One side will list ways in which people are better off; the other will list other ways in which they can be said to be worse off. But how can a judge decide, unless the criteria by which we are judging "better off" are agreed on? Having set those criteria, facts can come into play. If we accept that wealth is a fair measure of well-being: Has GDP risen since 2003? Is that figure reliable in the context of a post-war economy? How is wealth distributed among the people? There is plenty of ground for fruitful discussion and disagreement.

Propositions of Policy

A proposition of policy recommends taking action. It goes beyond merely justifying a value and additionally states that somebody should do something about it. For example, want to debate questions of poverty and low wages? Rather than a proposition of value like "Governments have a moral duty to tackle relative poverty," you would pose a proposition of policy like "The government should create a national minimum wage for all workers." Note that arguments about moral duty are still relevant to this debate, but it goes beyond that, bringing in practical considerations and all the possible consequences.

There are some useful ways of thinking about a proposition of policy to assess its strength.

Harm

You must prove that there is a problem, a need to change. At the very least, you must show that people will be better off in some way under your proposition. If people's response to your proposal is "so what?" then it is hard to convince them to act. The more significant the problem, the more people will understand the urgency to act. If people are dying, being injured, seeing their quality of life suffering, experiencing discrimination, make sure you highlight these when setting out your proposition.

Inherency

You need to show that the problem isn't going away by itself. If social attitudes are changing toward a group that used to face discrimination, why pass new laws to protect them? You need to analyze cause and effect—both of the problem you are trying to fix and of the solution you are putting forward.

Plan

You must provide a plan to solve the problem. Your plan sets forth the action you think necessary to deal with the problem. You need to include: *who* will take action, *what* action they will take, *how* it will be paid for, and *who* will make sure it is carried out. If you leave holes in your plan, opposition teams will be quick to suggest that the benefits you expect will not materialize.

Solvency

You need to show cause and effect. Prove how the plan will solve the problem or reduce the harm you presented at the start of your case.

Benefits

You should set out how, on balance, your plan provides additional advantages and benefits. These might not address the harm directly but discuss other good results of your plan, thus providing extra reasons to support the proposition. Perhaps changing the voting system to make it more representative would *also* increase participation in elections. That additional benefit is worth talking about.

Conclusion

These issues can be presented in different ways. You certainly shouldn't go through them one-by-one as you speak, ticking them off. But, as you begin your journey as a debater, be aware of how good propositions answer these questions quickly and effectively. A policy proposition needs to show how a policy will bring benefits. So you need to think of the values and the facts that help make your case.

Opposition may argue against your case in part or in full. They may seek to prove that the need for action is insignificant. They may focus on proving that it won't work. They may concede it would work, but show all sorts of negative consequences that outweigh the benefits you claim. Your duty is to listen carefully to how Opposition approach the debate and respond to what they actually say—not what you hoped, planned, or imagined they would say.

A good proposition guides the debate by making clear to all teams what they need to prove to win. It creates a fair, deep debate that all sides can engage with. Judges reward propositions that do a great job of starting a debate.

Important Concepts in This Chapter

1. There are two types of propositions: propositions of value (analysis debates) and propositions of policy (policy debates).

2. Propositions of value are statements of opinion, arrived at by analyzing a situation and making a judgment about it.

3. Propositions of policy are recommendations of action, suggesting a problem should be solved through a plan that is supported by values, is practical, and has beneficial effects.

EXERCISES

1. List five topic areas. Practice writing motions for analysis debates and policy debates. Try them and see the different types of debate they create.

2. Watch a clip of politicians debating on TV. Isolate the times when they are debating values, practicalities, and consequences.

KEY WORDS

analysis debate	practicalities
benefits	proposition
consequences	solvency
criteria	subjective
harm	This House
inherency	topic
motion	value
policy	

CHAPTER 7

Critical Thinking

Critical thinking is thinking about how you think. It involves looking at the beliefs and assumptions hidden beneath your everyday reasoning, understanding them better, and challenging them. Practically, it is the process of asking and answering questions as you work to understand how and why you come to the conclusions that you do. This is an essential skill for debate because debaters need to plan what they will say, think through opposing positions, and generate arguments that counter other teams' arguments. Debate is not just a discussion between two sides. Rather, it is a contest in which each side is trying to win by presenting a better argument and making the other team's arguments look less reasonable or weak.

This chapter describes the main parts of an argument and shows how critical thinking is necessary to create the strongest, most cohesive arguments possible. The chapter also describes how to recognize flawed arguments and use your opponents' flaws to your advantage.

Developing critical thinking skills is a great benefit of debate. The ability to think critically and analytically will help in your entire academic journey, whatever your discipline. You can use many approaches to become a better critical thinker:

- Comparing the viewpoints of other people to your own way of thinking

- Asking questions that challenge many perspectives, not just those you disagree with

- Understanding why some statements are correct and others are not

- Exploring the uncertainty of all knowledge

- Researching through critical reading and evaluation of ideas

- Understanding how problem solving works

- Establishing criteria for making judgments

- Presenting arguments in a constructive way

An entire other book would be needed to explore these fully. But don't be put off. At its simplest, as soon as you learn to argue and defend a position, you are a critical thinker. When you argue against another's position, you are a critical thinker. When you change your mind because of the arguments you hear, you are a critical thinker. When you explore how communication affects and influences other people, with an open mind, you are a critical thinker.

Constructing an Argument

Arguments in debate need to be thought out and easy to follow. Therefore, you must use critical thinking when constructing an argument.

An argument is something made to support a position. It starts with an *assertion*—a claim you want the judges and audience to accept—and follows it up with *reasoning* and *evidence*. Let us work through an example:

"Arming the police will reduce crime. Gun crime has risen by 30 percent over the last two years in our city. The police don't have the ability to respond because they lack fire-power: a baton is no match for a sawn-off shotgun. The Police Federation is lobbying for a change and we should give them the tools they need to protect us."

Notice how the evidence—gun crime rising by 30 percent, the Police Federation lobbying for a change—does not prove anything on its own. The argument needs to show that arming the police will lead to reductions in crime. At the moment, all it suggests is that gun crime has risen because the police are not armed. So let's strengthen it.

" . . . other cities that have armed patrols, like Aburga and Bibbor, have seen crime continue to fall. We have become a soft target for armed gangs. When we police with the same toughness as other cities, we will get the same results."

Notice how the extra evidence—from the cities of Aburga and Bibbor—is connected to two claims: that the city is a soft target and that toughness will create better results. Each of these claims can be disputed and needs to be demonstrated in the debate.

The combination of a single-sentence assertion, backed by logical reasoning and relevant evidence makes points stronger.

Analyzing Arguments

An argument must prove a claim. One trap that arguments can easily fall into is fallacy. Fallacies are faults in reasoning that damage arguments and indicate that our conclusions are not solid. Let's look at a few:

Begging the Question

When you try to make an argument by making a claim, then backing it up with reasoning that is assumed by the claim, you are *begging the question.* "The United States is losing its global power," a speaker says, "because the United States is in decline." Notice that the second half of the sentence just restates, in different language, the first half. The word *because* might make it feel like reasoning has taken place, but it hasn't.

Tautology

A tautology is defining a term by using the same term. "A bad law is a law that is bad" is true, but doesn't get us anywhere.

Straw Man

If you change an opponent's argument to make it easier to counter and then defeat the version you have created, you are only beating a *straw man.* Judges will not be impressed. "Scientific models of climate change have proved unreliable," avers Team A; Team B responds: "They don't believe in scientific models. Without science, we would still be relying on astrology and myth to predict the future. Is that how Team A sees the world?" This is a weak response. Team A aren't saying they don't believe in scientific models, but that these specific models involving climate change are unreliable.

Red Herring

A red herring is an irrelevant argument. In a debate about whether language classes should be compulsory in schools, making the point that science should be compulsory doesn't achieve anything.

Ad Hominem

This is Latin for "to the person." An ad hominem attack is when you direct your fire to the debater, not her argument. "What can a British debater know about colonialism?" "Perhaps if you were a little older, you would understand." "I can't believe we've just listened to seven men talking about abortion." All these are examples of using attacks on personal characteristics, rather than engaging with ideas.

Appeal to the People

Most people want something, so it should happen. This is a principle that has some attraction, and some political systems are based on it, but it is insufficient in debating. It is known as an *appeal to the people*. People sometimes change their minds. People are sometimes wrong in predicting what will work best for them. Some believe that people's decisions are subject to higher moral or political considerations. For example, millions of people eat fast food. Does that mean it is good for them? Are the health effects nobody's business but their own? Whether you think people should be stopped from following all their desires is a matter open to debate.

Appeal to Authority

An *appeal to authority* is when we claim that some expert or body has the final say on a question. Einstein and Gandhi said some wonderful, quotable things, but that does not give them the final word. The Supreme Court of the United States may have produced many fine judgments, but if the debate is happening in Malaysia, such judgments are hardly binding. In a debate, ideas should be weighed on their own merits.

Generalization

"Mothers love their children." Well, many do, but tragically some mothers abandon, abuse, sell, or even kill their children. If the debate is about people trafficking from war-torn countries, relying on this *generalization* may lead you to miss an important part of the debate. Being prepared to identify lots of different groups and to analyze them in different ways is a hugely valuable skill in debating.

Non Sequitur

This is Latin for "does not follow." *Non sequitur* describes an argument in which the conclusion does not follow from the reasoning. There are many ways to step into this trap, but in debate, it usually involves introducing changes in sense and meaning: Bill eats McDonald's hamburgers; McDonald's is a global business; therefore, Bill supports globalization.

Post Hoc

Post hoc is Latin for "after the fact." It is tempting to assume that because something happened immediately before a success, it caused it. "The government spent $20 million on road safety and therefore road deaths fell by 10 percent," Team A tell us. Perhaps. But deaths might have fallen by 10 percent anyway. Team A need to show us how the spending on road safety directly caused the fall in road deaths. There is an important difference between a cause and a correlation. If you plot "global average temperatures" against "global doughnut sales" since 1900, you will see a sharp increase in both. Does it prove that doughnuts cause global warming? No. It is not enough to present two data sets and assert that one caused the other. You need to use evidence and reasoning to prove it.

Your job, as a debater, is to present the best arguments you can construct. At the same time, you need to criticize the case constructed by the other side. As you get better at critical thinking, you will start to recognize faulty reasoning and use it to get deeper into each debate. Sometimes, fallacies will fit into neat groups like those listed above. Other times, they will be complex, sneakily hidden. What matters is not the names or categories they fall into, but your ability to explain what is wrong with the thinking of others; and, when they analyze your thinking, the ability to defend your arguments and demonstrate good reasoning.

Points of Information

Many types of debate have points of information. This is when debaters can interrupt a speaker on the other side with a question or short statement—when the speaker allows it. Points of information have a range of purposes: to clarify meaning, to point out inconsistencies, to demonstrate your continued relevance in a debate, to steer the speaker toward arguments you intend to make. Thinking critically is vital when using points of information. Teams need to use them strategically to help show the superiority of their case over that of other teams. Thinking and planning how and when to ask the right questions is all part of good debate technique. Answering a point of information well demonstrates your total command of the subject.

Making Points of Information

- Wait until the period during which points of information are allowed—normally after the first minute and before the last minute of the speech.

- Stand and say "point of information" or "on that point." Do not say anything else.

- If accepted, make sure the judges and audience can hear your point.

- Make your point in less than 15 seconds and sit down immediately.

- If the speaker does not accept your point or ignores you, please sit down again.

- Leave at least 15 seconds before seeking to ask another point.

- Try to make a point of information with every speaker.

Answering Points of Information

- When offered a point of information, say "no, thank you" or "accept the point."

- Take at least one point of information. If you do not, the judges will think you are being unfair to the other teams.

- Allow a reasonable opportunity for the point to be heard and understood.

- Answer the point directly and immediately before continuing. Saying "I'll come to that later" is not an acceptable response.

- When you ask and answer questions, you are trying to make the best impression you can on the judges. You want to appear fair, polite, intelligent, and sharp. You want to use each question as a way to demonstrate your team's superiority in the debate.

Cross-examination

In some debate formats, you have a short period of cross-examination. This is time at the end of constructive speeches where one team can ask questions of the other team. Critical thinking is key at this point because debaters must determine where they are going with their arguments in light of what the other team has said. The purpose of the cross-examination is not to argue with the other team but to gather information to support your case. So you must think carefully—and strategically—about both your questions and answers.

When You Are Asking Questions of the Other Team

- Face the audience when speaking. Do not face your opponent. Stand next to the speaker and slightly behind him or her.

- Ask simple questions that require "yes" or "no" answers as much as possible.

- Do not allow the person to answer with a long, involved explanation.

- Be polite when interrupting your opponent if her answers are too long.

- Do not allow your opponent to ask you questions. Politely remind him, "This is my cross-examination period."

- Do not make arguments during cross-examination.

- Use your opponent's answers from the cross-examination during your next speech.

When You Are Answering Questions from the Other Team

- Face the audience.

- If you need to explain your answer, tell your opponent you cannot answer "yes or no" and need to qualify your answer.

- Do not try to ask questions unless it is to clarify a question.

- When the time is finished, you do not need to answer any more questions.

- Think before you speak.

Important Concepts in This Chapter

1. Critical thinking is central to arguing a position and attacking an opponent's position effectively.

2. Sound arguments are the bedrock of debate. Every claim needs reasoning and evidence.

3. A fallacy is an unsound argument.

4. During points of information and cross-examination, a team can strengthen their arguments and weaken opponents' arguments through the use of critical thinking.

EXERCISES

1. Look for advertisements in magazines. See if you can spot any fallacies.

2. Find a newspaper article that you strongly disagree with. Try to construct a powerful set of arguments in favor of it. Use your critical thinking skills to get inside the head of somebody who disagrees with your views.

KEY WORDS

ad hominem

analysis

appeal to authority

appeal to the people

assertion

begging the question

claim

correlation

critical thinking

cross-examination

evidence

fallacy

generalization

non sequitur

post hoc

reasoning

red herring

straw man

tautology

CHAPTER 8

Research

In Chapter 2, we learned that when you make an assertion, you must prove it. You must provide evidence. This chapter suggests ways to gather and organize evidence so you can find it quickly during your debates.

The Importance of Evidence

You now know that you **must offer proof to complete an argument.** You also know that if a debater makes an argument without proof, the opposing teams will delight in challenging it. Debaters are not expected to be experts. Facts don't make arguments persuasive on their own. The team that offer evidence are at an advantage.

To prove an argument, it helps to have facts and information that support it. The only way to get these is through research. In some formats, like Worlds Style, you have very little preparation time and learn the topic just minutes before the debate. In others, you may have days or weeks to do research before you speak. However you debate, there is no substitute for developing a strong interest in current affairs, history, politics, economics, science, ethics—anything that has a bearing on how ideas affect the world. By reading the news, you will soon come up with plenty of ideas you can use for your next debate. Topics might include taxation, criminal justice, political systems, privacy, individual rights, social justice, labor policy, economic policy, international affairs, media, pop culture, education, health, family matters, sport, culture—anything!

Researching

Some of the best lessons you learn from debating will come through your research. When researching, don't just look for unusual topics to create new cases. Try to read the news wearing your critical thinker's glasses. Look at both sides of the argument—you never know which you will be assigned. Collect evidence that both supports and contradicts the position you currently hold. You need to research all sides of an issue to be ready for opponents and to be able to put a case strongly even if it is not your personal viewpoint.

What to Look for in Your Research

Evidence is any piece of information that helps a side prove its claim. Three of the most important types of evidence are:

Statistics

Whenever you want to prove significance, you can use data. The World Bank states that 1.2 billion of the world's people do not have access to clean water. Does that *prove* that Western governments should give aid to sub-Saharan Africa? No. In a debate about climate change, you might want to mention Tuvalu, where 80 percent of the island is seven feet or less above sea level. Does it prove that a global carbon tax should be implemented? No. But, in both cases, the statistic highlights the significance and urgency of the issue and lends weight to that case. Use data appropriately, remembering that statistics are open to question and criticism.

Examples

If you are making the case for legalizing drugs, perhaps you should look at countries that have legalized drugs and see what happened there. You may find that legalization had a range of positive and negative effects. Your job is to account for why a lot of the positives would happen, and the negatives be avoided in your model. It would certainly be strange to ignore these real-world examples without mentioning them. Be careful with examples, however: you can't just say "look what happened in Iraq" to oppose military intervention or "look what happened in Hiroshima" to oppose nuclear weapons and think you have won the point. You need to link your examples well and show why they are relevant to the debate.

Testimonials or Expert Opinions

Sometimes experts have opinions that support your position. This is called a *testimonial*. Scientists working for the United Nations in their millennium ecosystem assessment indicated that destruction of ocean fisheries posed the greatest worldwide danger of starvation. You could use this opinion to support a case about denying oil-drilling rights in coastal areas or for the reform of global fisheries treaties. You are not guaranteed victory, but expert opinion does force other teams to try to explain why the experts might be wrong or why their opinion is less important than you claim.

Finding the Evidence

Most of us rely on the Internet as the quickest, easiest way to gain access to the largest possible volume of information.

For most of us, Google and Wikipedia are a reflex first home for research. Remember, you have to be careful about how you use these tools. Just because someone, somewhere writes something doesn't make it true! Websites may not go through the extensive editorial and review process that many print sources do. Ask yourself the following questions:

- Who are the authors of the site?

- What are their qualifications?

- Might they have a bias?

- Does the site exist to advocate a specific position?

- When was the information last updated?

To broaden your knowledge, try reading news from different parts of the world. Find out what people across the political spectrum are currently thinking and talking about.

To deepen your knowledge in a particular area, be prepared to spend some time in the library. Books, specialized magazines, scholarly journals, and other off-line sources can help you delve deeply into your topic. The better your background understanding of world history, the more perspective you can bring to contemporary international conflicts. Insights from the great philosophers can help you bring multiple ethical viewpoints to an issue, rather than simply weighing up the consequences.

Reading and Collating Evidence

Once you find the evidence you are looking for, you need to put it into a usable form. Some of you might just want to read to improve your background knowledge. But, if you would like to have the information available during a debate, you will need to create a case file. The Worlds Style format does not allow you to access the Internet during preparation time—but it does allow you to refer to written material. So, when you find something useful, make a copy, highlight important areas, and put it into a folder.

The best way to organize evidence is to divide it into subject areas so that you can find it quickly and easily. Read through the evidence regularly and become familiar with your files and adjust how information is organized if necessary.

In some types of debate, policy debate, for instance, you are expected to read your printed evidence. This is called *direct quotation*. In Worlds Style, many speakers do not carry written evidence with them at all, instead relying on what they may have learned from many sources over the course of their reading and learning.

Assessing Evidence

You should not try to use all the evidence you have. Debating does not measure knowledge, but persuasiveness. Persuasiveness involves making arguments. Arguments are supported by evidence. You must make choices, taking the best evidence and using it skillfully. How do you know which evidence is best? Here are three tests:

1. **Is it recent?** How old is the evidence? Timeliness is not an issue in some areas, such as philosophy or religion. When dealing with current events, however, the judges will usually trust evidence that is contemporary. If your research suggests that an international treaty will struggle to gain international support, but 100 countries just signed it the day before the debate, your evidence is weakened and should not be used. Similarly, theories of international relations based on Cold War thinking from the twentieth century may need more time now to justify than they would have in the 1980s. Situations and laws change, so you must be prepared to defend the timeliness of your evidence.

2. **Is it relevant?** Does the evidence prove the point? Your evidence must be directly related to the claim it is supporting. "The United States has had five presidents since 1980" does not prove in any way "The United Kingdom should abolish the monarchy and have an elected

president." It is a piece of information about presidents, but it is not relevant to the point being made.

3. Is it reliable? Are the sources trustworthy? You want to quote somebody with expertise, training, or experience in the field. Journalists are paid to write—you should be slow to give them authority. Their opinions are not facts. When evaluating the reliability of a source, ask yourself:

   a. Is the source in a position to know the truth?

   b. Was the source a witness to the event?

   c. Does the source have a bias?

You don't have to dismiss every source who cannot be proved to be objective. You just have to be aware of the biases and sensitivities required to get through to the facts.

Organizing Evidence

Organizing evidence is necessary to present a strong case. It involves separating data into individual items and being specific about connecting that evidence to the right arguments. Perhaps you have found lots of data about nuclear power station safety and you are debating energy. It isn't enough to list facts you have learned. You need to spend time thinking about how specific facts relate to individual points you want to raise.

The quality of research can be a determining factor in who wins debates. Knowledge itself is of no value in debating but, used to support powerful arguments, it is very helpful indeed. One of the great educational achievements in debating is its power to motivate students to research, to learn, and to apply their learning.

Important Concepts in This Chapter

1. Debate requires good research skills to gather evidence that you can use at a moment's notice.

2. Statistics, examples, testimonials, and expert opinions are good types of evidence.

3. To evaluate evidence, determine if it is recent, relevant, and reliable.

EXERCISES

1. Read an article by an environmental expert. Be able to state the qualifications of the source. How many individual pieces of information can you find in the article?

2. Find several articles on a topic that interests you. Cut and paste the evidence onto different sheets of paper. Find the evidence that supports the case in favor. Then put together the evidence that opposes that case.

3. Find the three types of evidence we discussed—statistics, examples, and testimonials—in a newspaper article.

KEY WORDS

direct quotation	relevant
evidence	reliable
examples	statistics
recent	testimonial

CHAPTER 9
Refutation

This chapter discusses one of the most crucial parts of good debate—*refutation*. Before refutation takes place, the two teams are really just presenting what they want you to know about their side of the issue. This can be frustrating for judges and an audience unless the two sides begin to interact and spell out where they disagree with each other. Refutation is where you show that your argument is stronger than your opponents'. Refutation almost always involves countering the evidence that someone has presented, blurring link between evidence and argument, or ripping apart the argument's reasoning. In earlier chapters, you learned how to make your arguments stronger. This chapter shows you how to challenge your opponents' arguments successfully.

Repeat, Rebut, Replace

Refutation is a process that can be divided into three steps:

Repeat the argument that you are going to refute. The judges and audience need to know where exactly your disagreement begins and ends. Make your opponents' point the strongest you possibly can before showing how and why it should be rejected. This is important. Debating is not about pretending other people always make bad points, but the ability to deal effectively with good points and still put forward a convincing alternative.

Rebut the argument. Explain what is wrong with it. Look to the assertion itself, the reasoning or the evidence. Find tensions between them. Check for premises that have not been proved.

Replace the argument with your own. It is not enough to be destructive. The judges need to know what you think and see if you are capable of constructing a more persuasive argument.

Putting the three together, you might say: "Their second point was that governments cannot enforce restrictions on smoking in public places. They gave the example of Great Britain. But, in fact, Britain has succeeded in creating smoke-free environments and seen a continued fall in the number of smokers every year since the ban. Governments can make public places free of smoke by law if they have the right enforcement mechanism."

Make sure that your refutation is organized and that it includes all three steps. Make sure the judges can follow your presentation, that your diagnosis of weakness is right, and that your alternative is presented in a winning way.

Refutation Strategy

Knowing the repeat-rebut-replace process, you still need to think about how and when to deploy it. Debates are not just a list of arguments and responses. Each side is presenting a case, a story of the debate according to their viewpoint. Thus, you need to be selective and strategic about your refutation.

Use Signposting

Signposting is when, at the beginning of a speech, you tell everyone the organization and order of what you will say. It is like a road map, telling the judges, other debaters, and the audience what they can expect so your speech will be easy to follow. One approach is simply to outline the points you intend to rebut. A better method is giving an overview of where you disagree as part of your introduction. You need to point out the moment in the story where you part company with the other side. "Opposition claimed that smoking bans are illiberal and unenforceable. We dispute that and intend to show they can work and help to foster greater free-dom for all." Note the lack of detail—that will come later.

Create Clash

Clash is a word debaters use to describe moments when debaters are dealing directly with each other's arguments. In a good debate, this will be a high proportion of the time! You want to clash with your opponents' arguments and demonstrate engagement. But time is limited, so you need to be selective about which arguments to choose. So, you must prioritize their arguments that were:

- **The best.** Judges will reward speakers who can deal with the toughest points not the easiest ones. It may be tempting to take a point that is obviously wrong and spend a lot of time reminding the judges of it. Try to avoid that temptation. Focus on those arguments that do your case the most damage and do your best to show why they are not as strong as your opponents believe them to be.

- **The longest.** If you find it hard to judge which were the strongest, use the length of time spent on each argument as a guide. In a seven-minute speech, if arguments 2, 3 and 4 got six minutes, whereas 1 and 5 got twenty seconds each, then the speaker's own priorities are made clear.

Group Arguments

If a team makes relevant arguments that are ignored by the other teams, judges will give them credit. If they are met with silence, even flawed arguments can carry weight. So, debaters must listen and then choose carefully where to respond. One way to achieve this is to *group* arguments together. Perhaps the opposition has identified several ways in which implementing your policy might prove difficult. Then put them together: "Opposition say compulsory drug treatment will be expensive, there will be loopholes, that people won't register and the police won't enforce it. We accept there will be additional cost; but the cost comes because we are equipping the police to enforce it, to force people to register and to fill the loopholes." In this example, we have grouped together four pieces of rebuttal and answered them with a single point—showing the connections.

Use "Even if"

Judges don't have to accept every tiny detail of everything you say for you to win a debate. In fact, many debates are very close and decided on relatively small differences. So, you need to give judges as many opportunities as possible to accept your version of events. A great tool for achieving this is "even if." To see how it works, let's apply it to the last example of rebuttal we used: "Opposition say it will be expensive, there will be loopholes, that people won't regis-ter and the police won't enforce it. We *don't accept* it will be expensive, as it will create long-term savings in reduced crime, but *even if* it were, it would be a price worth paying for equipping the police to enforce it, to force people to register, and to fill the loopholes." Note the improvement here: rather than conceding one point to rebut three, we have created a position where all four are defended. But we have shown that *even if* the judges are unpersuaded by our cost point, they still have reason to support us. This is smart strategy and maximizes the opportunity for judges to agree with us.

Attacking a Case

So far in this chapter, we have looked at how to refute indi-vidual arguments and how to apply strategy to refuting arguments. Now, let us turn to the big target: the overall case. It is easy to get bogged down in the detail of indi-vidual points and miss what is glaringly obvious—that the whole case presented has fundamental flaws. Much more credit is to be gained from noticing, diagnosing, and attacking a fatal problem with the case than picking over individual points. Here are three big ones to look out for:

Solvency

If a team's case doesn't pass the test it sets itself, then it is in big trouble. If the proposition is that the UN should send a military force into North Korea, yet the Government teams concede that the consent of the North Korean government is necessary to enter, then the proposition isn't going to work. Missing this or mentioning it in passing before diving into deep meditations on the previous success or failure of UN missions would be a mistake for their opponents.

Consequences

If a team claims that they only want to debate an issue in principle, regardless of how it would play out in reality, then they are in big trouble. Benefits and costs are relevant in debating. If you want to spend money on one project, you need to spend less on something else, tax someone, or borrow money from someone. If you want to go to war, you will kill innocent people. These costs cannot be ignored, wished away, or ruled out of order. Opponents should spend time highlighting the consequences of action versus the consequences of their alternative, and create a compelling cost/benefit analysis that their argument is superior.

Criteria

In an analysis debate, the Government must set criteria, or standards of measurement, that allow the question to be judged. The Opposition does not have to accept these and may provide better criteria of their own. Often, a team will set a burden for themselves that is subtly easier to meet than if their opponents had chosen it. Opposition must be quick to notice any unfairness in the criteria established by the Government and be happy to challenge them. For example, if Government say "the true standard of whether the Iraq war was successful is GDP in Iraq," Opposition should be quick to point out that mortality rates and life expectancy have a place in the calculation.

Important Concepts in This Chapter

1. Refutation is showing opponents' arguments to be weaker than yours.

2. The basic process of refutation can be summed up as repeat-rebut-replace.

3. Techniques used in refutation strategy include signposting, creating clash, grouping arguments, and using "even if."

4. In refuting an opponent's case, debaters should watch out for solvency, consequences, and unfair criteria.

EXERCISES

1. Read a newspaper editorial. Think of reasons why you might support the editorial and why you might reject it. Give a speech about both sides.

2. One student should give a five-minute speech. A second student should then, without preparation, give a three-minute refutation. Practice looking for solvency, consequences, and unfair criteria.

KEY WORDS

clash	refutation
consequences	repeat
criteria	replace
even if	signposting
grouping	solvency
premise	standards
rebut	strategy

CHAPTER 10

Tournaments and Judges

This chapter prepares you for the challenge of putting your debating skills to the test in competition. Debate tournaments are a great way to expand your horizons, improve your skills, and enjoy debating against people from other schools, even other countries. You will get the chance to encounter new arguments, test yourself, learn more, and develop your talents. Hopefully, you will come away excited about debate and ready for more.

Some students are satisfied with debating in the classroom, but others enjoy tournaments, which allow competition between schools. Every year thousands of tournaments are held worldwide in various formats. Teams that want to be champions try to debate against as many schools as possible. The more experience they gain, the more prepared they will be for the championships.

Tournaments

As a *novice* debater, you will probably not be able to show up and win a debate tournament. Nevertheless, it is a great idea to attend and take part. Even if you lose every round, by watching how experienced debaters speak and compete you can learn a huge amount.

Some tournaments have a special prize for the best novice team to recognize excellence among new debaters and to encourage them. Some tournaments allow *floor speeches* after the final, whereby anyone can stand up and make a short speech while the audience is waiting for the judges to confirm the result. You have nothing to lose. Take every opportunity to speak in front of an audience.

Tournaments usually are held on weekends. Most charge an entrance fee for each team, plus you have to consider the expenses of travel, meals, and accommodation if it is not provided. Some tournaments require you to bring a judge for every two teams.

Most tournaments divide into *preliminary rounds* in which everybody competes and *break rounds* in which the best teams fight it out for overall victory. Formats differ, but in World Style, the first preliminary round is drawn at random, after which teams are assigned against others who have a similar record in the tournament. This helps to ensure that debates are competitive and teams well matched. At the end of the preliminary rounds, the teams with the best records progress to the break rounds, which are straight knockout debates until the final.

Sample schedule

Registration	09:00	Re-registration	09:00
Briefing	10:00	Round 4	10:30
Round 1	10:30	Lunch	12:00
Lunch	12:00	Round 5	13:30
Round 2	13:30	Semifinals	16:00
Round 3	16:30	Final	18:00
Dinner and Social	19:00	Party	20:00

Some tournaments also hold a final for the best teams whose members speak English as a Second Language. This is called the ESL final. The ESL final of a tournament is only open to those who did not grow up speaking English. The World University Debating Championships (WUDC) has a separate category of English as a Foreign Language (EFL) and holds not only an ESL final but quarter-finals and semifinals as well.

If you are looking for opportunities to debate internationally, ask whether a tournament has an ESL final. It is a good way to match up against non-native speakers in front of a big audience, even if you do not reach the overall final. But remember that non-native speakers of English can and do win debating tournaments. ESL and EFL categories are just additional opportunities for recognition.

Large tournaments like the World University Debating Championships can have hundreds of teams competing from more than 50 countries. Smaller tournaments may have only a dozen from local schools.

Judges must determine the winners and losers of each debate according to common rules decided in advance. The standards required of judges are normally reinforced at a briefing at the start of the day. Formats differ but, in Worlds Style, you normally have at least three judges for each debate, with as many as nine for a grand final in a major tournament. After a debate, the judges fill out a ballot, which is returned to the tournament director to record the results. The judges then give oral feedback to the debaters, explaining why they gave the result they did and suggesting ways each team could improve in future debates.

Tournament competition is exciting and fun. It is also one of the best educational opportunities of your life. Not only will you improve your spoken English and learn critical thinking skills, through international competition you can gain broader perspectives, meet new people, experience different cultures, and make great friends along the way. It improves your resume and gives you something impressive to discuss at job interviews. More important, it creates relationships that can last a lifetime and offers learning experiences that are hard to match. We hope you discover the same enjoyment that we have found.

Important Concepts in This Chapter

1. Competing in debate tournaments is an excellent way to become a better debater and improve your English language skills.

2. Tournaments have many different formats, but most divide into preliminary rounds and break rounds.

3. The best novice team sometimes receives a special prize.

4. Bigger tournaments sometimes have an ESL final or EFL final to reward debaters for whom English is not a native language.

5. Judges must be fair in their decisions and also provide constructive feedback to debaters.

EXERCISES

Participate in as many debates as you possibly can.

Take opportunities to adjudicate, to watch debates, and to learn from others.

KEY WORDS	
break	novice
EFL	preliminary
ESL	rounds
	tournaments
feedback	World University
floor speech	Debating Championships
judge	Worlds Style

Debate Transcript

The best way to get a sense of how to debate is to do it. If you can't do it, watch it, and if you can't watch it live, look for debates online. This transcript is another option. Without the pressure of having to follow and understand a debate live, you can read the text and get a sense of how debaters try to organize and deliver a speech.

Below is a transcript of the first two speeches from the final of the World University Debating Championships 2013. You will notice small areas where the text says [unclear . . .]. This is normal when we watch debates. Noises, coughs, mistakes in sentence construction happen frequently. This is a judge's eye view—it cannot be a definitive account of every single word the speakers said but only what can actually be heard. You can go online, watch the debate, and see how much you can follow. Be assured that inability to hear every word is not a language barrier issue for you the listener, but the responsibility of the speakers.

This is a Worlds Style debate. As you read, remember that the speakers had only 15 minutes preparation time; remember that they didn't choose their side of the debate; and imagine the nerves as you consider that an audience of several hundred people was watching. If you want to see the whole debate, it is available as WUDC Berlin 2013 Open Final on YouTube.

Other great search terms and sources for debate include:

"WUDC" for debates from the World Universities Debating Championships.

"EUDC," "WUPID," "LSE Open" are fruitful terms for finding other Worlds Style debates with lots of speakers of English as a second language.

Professor Alfred Snider of the University of Vermont has a superb collection of debate videos at http://debatevideoblog .blogspot.co.uk

Analysis Points

These are the first two speeches of a Worlds Style debate (Chapter 5).

The Prime Minister gives a preview of the speech, telling us what the speech is seeking to prove. The body of his speech then focuses on what is right (principles) and harms (consequences) (Chapter 4).

The Prime Minister puts forward a policy and claims the policy will have benefits (Chapter 6).

Both speakers accept points of information, answering them directly (Chapter 7).

The Leader of the Opposition uses a grabber to get our attention and organizes the speech to make it easy for us to follow (Chapter 4).

The Leader of the Opposition refutes points made by the Prime Minister, repeating, rebutting, and replacing; he uses signposting and "even if" arguments (Chapter 9).

The Leader of the Opposition refers to the point of information offered by his partner, demonstrating teamwork (Chapter 1).

World Universities Debating Championships 2013

Motion: This House would not allow religious communities to expel members on the basis of views or actions that contradict doctrinal teaching.

Prime Minister

Ladies and Gentlemen, I'm proud to say that at the final of Berlin Worlds it's the case from government that religious communities should embrace dissent.

We will seek to prove two things today on Government today, the first one that for a religious community to expel someone who simply disagrees with them or acts slightly outside what they believe at that time in their religious history is outside the scope of what a religion has a right to do or what a religion can punish a person for.

Secondly, we are going to show you that there are actually going to be more benefits than harms to religious communities in this debate. What are we talking about? We're talking about situations such as when a young woman in a religious community has an abortion, when a young man comes out as gay, when people experience particularly tolerant viewpoints or dispute particular aspects of that religion, that that religious community cannot simply expel them or eject them—families are not allowed to throw them out on the basis of what has occurred here. We think that this will really apply to what are quite conservative religious communities because they are the ones that typically conduct these actions today.

So, the first point, then, that we bring to you: we think that this is far beyond what a religion has a right to do in terms of punishment for an individual. The first point is that the role religion plays in society is of the kind of nature that it means religions are fundamentally in the public sphere. Why do we think this? We think that religious communities or religious institutions are fundamentally the center of social interaction for their people. It's often simply true that people go to church and they interact in that circumstance. It's true that when the Islamic bells [sic] ring, people go to prayer; they will then often interact afterwards. We figure that means that communities cohere around these religions. Secondly, we see that religion is generally the center of national culture in many of these places and these communities. That means it plays a role at a particular level in society which is public. Finally, we think religion typically likes to extend itself into public discourse and have an influence on society. We think that that means it takes on a particular role and identifies itself as public. Finally, we think, and this flows into the second point I am going to make—religion has a particular power over people that makes it on a public level.

Point of information (Opposition Whip): Sir, how do you anticipate these people will be treated if they remain in these religious communities?

Well, as we're going to tell you, adjustment and reconciliation is a normal part of human existence, and we think that even though initially these people reject and dislike the people who act outside what they believe is true, typically they will realize that those people still fundamentally agree with the religious views on a broad level and will actually come to adjust and accept those people within their communities—that has happened in religious communities throughout history, it happens with us when we meet people who disagree, it's normal and we say that will continue to happen.

But going back to the point I was making just before, we think that for a religion to do this to an individual is the most destructive action that a public community can have. Why do we think that? Firstly, we say that it necessarily condemns this person to Hell—it is the strongest form of rejection that a living religion can actually do to a person. It says that you are so outside the scope of what we can do that there is no [unclear . . .] our religious views—you are going to Hell, good-bye.

Secondly we say, and this is particularly important, because this person has no choice—they did not opt in to this religion because they were born into it, within their community, they were raised with those values from the very first day, often they were baptized as a child. It means that they do not have that decision-making power—that means they've been imbued with those from an early age and it is usually at an early age that they start to express these views, that they start to feel there might be things about them that are distinct from this religion as well. Secondly we say that this person probably didn't choose the circumstances that led them to disagree with that religion. We say obviously being gay is not a choice—if you are gay and that religion doesn't accept you, we think that means you don't choose to do that or be in the religion at all. So we say that this is unfair action for a religious community to take to a person. particularly given that we do think that religion can be valuable.

Which leads me nicely to my second point—we think that this can be particularly valuable to religions themselves— that it can be a positive catalyst for change within the religious communities themselves. This problem with religion today—the nature of religion is such that it is bound by Scripture, it is bound by history and the fact that it tends to be stagnant in terms of how it moves. Often the people that have control over religions are particularly conservative members of them as well, because they are the ones that adhere to the values that the broad majority agree with and we think they are likely to be more conservative.

Point of information (Deputy Leader of the Opposition): Would you oblige someone to hang out with a person who their wife or kid [unclear . . .]?

Well, no, but rules and societal things exist to deal with that sort of situation. Of course, you're allowed to divorce a person [unclear . . .] generally communities generally accept that person so we don't think that is particularly applicable to this debate.

Okay, so what does that mean—that religions exist in a particular conservative way; usually societies struggle to adapt to the pace of change of society. When society liberalizes as it typically does, they do not adjust to the inevitable change that occurs when new technologies are invented and we have greater connectivity with the rest of the world that reveals particular different values. They struggle to accept and adjust with that. We say it has been particularly bad recently as the pace of change has started to move fast particularly in terms of [unclear . . .] in the world. This is bad firstly for the communities themselves because it separates them from those societies, it means that they choose not to interact, more often than not, with other people and we think that is bad for them. Secondly it fundamentally undermines the overall purpose of religions, typically religions want to do good in the world, whether that's spreading their own doctrines or doing the things that charitable Christians, for example, providing welfare for people in exchange for being able to spread that religion. If they can't adjust to society, they are likely to not be able to do the good in the world that they want to.

So why is it, in this instance, that we think these people would be a good mechanism for change? The first thing to be said here is that people that [unclear . . .] to religion are going to be more comfortable and more likely to express themselves and their views within these communities. If you are gay, you are far more likely to come out to your religious community if they know they can't reject you. You're more likely to express viewpoints that you have. We say that's true for extreme cases but it also you don't get the chilling influence, you don't get the fear of people expressing slightly controversial views or slightly different views to the rest of the community so that means you get that broad acceptance there as well. We think that, therefore, and I made this point in response to a point of information, that you get these sort of forced interactions that lead to tolerance. When people disagree, religions are bad at tolerating that disagreement—typically religions are likely to immediately reject people on the basis that it violates something they have always believed their entire lives— that is a very short-term action with short-term thinking, we say that often if they are forced to interact with them and forced to live with those viewpoints that the person actually does look forward [unclear . . .] is still very much like them and therefore they tend to reconcile themselves and their beliefs with that person and with their views as well. For all these reasons, we are very proud to propose.

Leader of the Opposition

Madam Chair, you might view it as odious that a religious community doesn't want a gay person in their congregation, but your distaste for that does not mean that you have a right to force that religious community to accept them.

Furthermore, at Opening Opposition, we are going to argue that forcing that community to accept that individual has harms both for that person and for the progress of that group. So: three issues in this speech, with rebuttal and substantive integrated. Firstly, freedom of association and the right of communities to define their members; secondly, harms to the vulnerable individuals; and thirdly, that this is a very bad way to change religion.

So firstly, to freedom of association, and we heard from the Prime Minister that somehow the private institutions of religion cross some threshold into the public sphere that means that they are public property. We said this was absolutely ridiculous. The fact that lots of people in a community go to a church does not mean that that church is an institution of that entire community. It is not an institution of the entire community because not everyone is allowed to be a member of the church to begin with. If you turn up on your first day at church and profess that you have no faith in God, then that church can legitimately reject you, so what does it matter if you believe on your first day and then come back a week later and say you don't believe; that community still has the right to expel you. Then he told us "ah, but they insert themselves into discourse and into the public sphere"—we think that these sorts of religions that you talk about that heavily prize their ability to exclude members are the ones that don't particularly intervene in the state, that are happy to accept a quid pro quo that they don't try to influence national politics in return for the state not messing with them. What do we say, in the alternative, about this freedom of association? We say that religious groups are no different to any other group; that they can exclude people on any criteria they want, even subjective, even if that is based on belief in God, and that a particular act, such as homosexuality, is a sin. We would give the examples of political parties, where if an individual undermines that message, they would be legitimate in expelling that person. Dom gave you an excellent example in a point of information, that you wouldn't force an adulterer to hang out with that person [unclear . . .] moral judgments are allowed, to decide the company that they keep.

Let's turn now to the harm to the religious communities that is inflicted by this. What you are doing is making people sit in church with people that they know make a mockery of their beliefs and constantly contradict them; people that question whether God exists, question whether God is all good, or all knowing. That is incredibly harmful for all the other people in that congregation. Even if it is something like someone being gay, or a priest marrying a gay person, or being an adulterer, this also is incredibly harmful to those other religious people's ability to actualize their belief in freedom of religion—because they will have a belief that what they are doing in allowing that person to continue in their religious institution is being complicit in their sin, that they have not succeeded in stopping that person, and that they have not expressed the disapproval by expelling them from that group. The harm to the religious people in that instance is enormous—things like forcing them to watch gay people be married by rogue priests that now can't be kicked out by the Catholic church—because they believe that they will be punished into eternity in Hell because they are complicit in this sin that you are foisting upon them.

Let's turn to the opposite right here which is the harm to the excluded group; and we heard from the Prime Minister that they have no choice to religion. That is absolutely not true. You can be dunked in a baptismal font, but that doesn't mean very much to the people who then go on to question their religion, and they are welcome to leave at any time—they absolutely do have choice of religion.

Next we heard they have no choice over the characteristic which makes them hated by the religious community; well they used the very selective example of homosexuality; in the instance of all other sins, like adultery, you do have control over those things, and this model is going to force a lot of people who are just making choices that make a mockery of those religions, to carry on in them.

All right, the second argument I want to look at is the harm to the individual. We say that these individuals are going to be more harmed in the group than out, because we are not talking about little tiny disagreements in today's debate, we are talking about rather large disagreements between them and the rest of that congregation, the sorts of things that aren't just going to be all right after time like the Prime Minister said, because being gay might be against the fundamental tenets of that religion. So what we say is that these communities are always going to have a very deep desire to get rid of that person, and that is going to manifest itself in making it as unpleasant as possible for that person to be there, not just saying that homosexuality is a sin, but saying that it is an abomination and bullying them in every possible opportunity to get out. And I'll take Closing.

Point of Information (Member of the Government): A gay man is never going to become a priest in a church and encourage more liberal attitudes if he is kicked out at the bottom rung. Don't you agree that means that the religion might never actually reflect what the majority of people in that community want it to reflect?

I'm going to turn to rights as a bad way to change religion in my third argument, but the unfortunate thing is that you don't have a right to expose people to contradictory ideas just because you would prefer that people had your set of liberal values. It's quite [unclear . . .] for them to continue to be conservative into eternity.

So turning back to the harms on the individual: we say that when the church can't externalize that problem, or force that individual out of the church that they think is committing a constant sin, they now have the incentive to make them internalize that hatred, make them hate themselves for being gay, because that's the only way they can mete out sufficient punishment to that person, in order to make them act in conformity with what the church would want. As a result of that, it's going to be much harder [unclear...] to reconcile their religious belief with being Catholic, with their sexuality, when the church has an incentive to make them hate themselves for it because they can't simply kick them out for it. We think that this model massively harms those individuals.

The last argument I want to look at in this debate is about why this is a bad way to change those religions. Because we heard from the Prime Minister that conservative members control the church; we absolutely think that doesn't change under this model. We then heard that they will see that the person who is sinning is not very different to them. We think it could also have the opposite effect. It could confirm their worst stereotypes, if, for example, if someone were promiscuous, that that could confirm their worst stereotypes of that group that they already hate, and that would be a massive harm in this debate. But furthermore, even if they are like them in every other respect in believing in God, it only takes one unforgiven sin to not enter into heaven anyway, so we don't think this is something they are going to lie together over and sing "Kum ba yah" over.

What did we tell you about why this is a bad way to change religion? We would say that changing religion is more likely when discourse is dispassionate, when you are not seen as [unclear . . .] forcing your view upon them, they are more likely to respond to rational arguments about whether or not they should liberalize. Secondly, they are more likely to change if they don't think that this is being prejudged by the state, if they don't feel that they particularly are being victimized because they are religious. So, because we think that religions absolutely do have this right, and it harms the individuals and any change you would achieve, we are very proud to oppose.

Note-taking Shorthand

You may want to develop your own symbols so you can flow faster. Here are some of my favorite shorthand abbreviations I use to flow a debate:

agent of action	A of A		dropped	[D]
because	b/c		enforcement	Enf
better	B		evidence	ev
billion	bil		funding	fund
contention	C		greater than	>
cost benefit analysis	CBA		impact	imp
			increase	↑
criteria	Crit		inherency	INH
decrease	↓		is/equals	=
disadvantage	DA		less than	<
dollars	$			

linear	/	should	s/
link	L	significance	sig
million	mil	solvency	sol
not equal	≠	status quo	SQ
not	∅	therefore	∴
number	#	thousand	K or M
observation	O, obs	topicality	T
policy	P, pol	uniqueness	U
quantify	Q	voting issue	VI
question	?	with	w/
should not	s/n	without	w/o

Sample Outlines

I. Observation #1

    A. Point about Observation #1

    B. Point about Observation #1

    C. Point about Observation #1

    D. Point about Observation #1

        1. Detail on Point D

        2. Detail on Point D

II. Observation #2

    A. Point about Observation #2

    B. Point about Observation #2

III. Observation #3

    A. Point about Observation #3

    B. Point about Observation #3

    C. Point about Observation #3

        1. Detail on Point C

        2. Detail on Point C

IV. Plan

V. Observation #4

    A. Point about Observation #4

You may choose many different ways to get the attention and interest of the audience. Sometimes the affirmative will give a greeting or general thank you to begin parliamentary debates. A story or example could also be given. Some teams prefer to first state a philosophy about their case before the greeting. The introduction should end by stating the resolution, so the audience knows what will be debated. In some debates, the first words of the affirmative may be a simple statement of the resolution being debated.

You may want to number the points of your case throughout the rest of the debate so that everyone can follow your arguments easily. You may call these specific points either **contentions** or **observations.**

What each of these observations and points should include:

I. **Observation One—Resolutional Analysis (RA)**

   A. In this main point of your case you want to let everyone know the position you are taking on the resolution. Additionally, you want to provide the following:

   B. Definition of key terms—Not every word needs to be defined. Only the words that might be important for the debate need a definition. The definitions must be reasonable to be fair to the other team. Some teams will even provide the source of the definitions.

C. Resolution type—If you believe that the resolution is a policy resolution, tell the judge which words in the resolution allow you to argue this. In a policy resolution, you would analyze the action verb that is in the resolution that makes it a call to action.

D. Burdens—This is what the affirmative team must meet to prove their case and win the debate.

E. Decision rule—This is how you explain to the judges how they should be judging the round or on what basis they will determine who did the better job of debating.

II. **Observation Two—Needs**

A. Harms—What bad things are happening right now due to the current state of affairs or current policy that kill or injure people or other living creatures? You may also want to point out how a value is also involved.

B. Significance—There are two different types of significance, quantitative and qualitative. **Quantitative significance** provides numbers (X number of people are being hurt) while **qualitative significance** provides why the value is important (why protecting Y is important). You may decide to prove both or only one type of significance in a debate.

III. **Observation Three—Inherency (attitudes or laws)**

    A. Attitudinal Inherency—A state of mind or feeling. What attitudes are causing the problem? Examples are greed, ignorance, apathy or prejudice.

    B. Structural Inherency—What laws could be improved to help stop the harm from happening?

IV. **Plan**—The affirmative has a burden to show how they could stop or reduce the harm.

    A. Agent of action—Who will be the one to pass the law or enforce the law?

    B. Mandate—What will the law do to stop or reduce the harm?

    C. Funding—How will we pay for the plan?

    D. Enforcement—How will we enforce the plan?

V. **Observation Four—Solvency**

    A. How does the plan work to stop or reduce the harm? Usually, you would provide analysis and evidence to support this position.

VI. **Advantages**—Are there any other good things that will come from the plan (in addition to solving the harm)?

Sample Case Development and Outline for Values-Based Debates

With a value resolution, such as in Lincoln-Douglas style debate, the affirmative does not have to present a plan but rather just provide evidence to support the claim that is made by the resolution. However, many people in the United States believe the best way to prove a value is to provide a policy since most policies support a value, like health care for all or abolishing capital punishment. The structure below is for a resolution of value that is not proved through a policy.

I. **Observation One**

    A. Definition of key terms—Which words need to be explained to clarify the debate?

    B. Resolution type—Which terms in the resolution ask us to make a value judgment or comparison?

    C. Appropriate context—Under what time and space conditions should we be able to make the value judgment? Explain why it is the most appropriate context.

    D. The value being debated—Why is the value of your case the highest value?

E. Criteria—When we will know when we have enough evidence to prove the position? This is a measurement of the value by an objective standard.

F. Decision rule—What is the ground of the other team? This is how the judge should be able to decide who did the better of job of debating.

II. Observation Two

A. Provide examples or proof of the criteria being met in the context of the debate with as many contentions as you have time for.

III. Observation Three

A. Provide examples or proof of the criteria being met in the context of the debate with as many contentions as you have time for.

Below is a sample outline of a persuasive speech without evidence citations to show what a speech outline could look like. Note that it is not a speech written out word-for-word, but just an outline to use when giving a speech.

1. **Introduction:** Tell the story of the movie, Water World, where actor Kevin Costner stars as the hero who must live in a world after the polar ice caps have melted and earth is almost completely covered with water. Although the movie was science fiction, it paints a picture of what could be if we don't do something about global warming.

Because the green house effect traps heat, the world will be faced with many new environmental disasters. Yet, if we take strong and decisive actions we may be able to save our planet for our children.

2. **Thesis Statement:** Today, I urge you to help stop the dangers of global warming.

3. **Preview:** First, I will prove the increasing problems we can expect from rising temperatures. Second, I will explore the many causes for this threat. Finally, we will discover what we can do to slow down the damage to our world.

4. **Body**

   I. The worldwide problems of global warming will increase in significance.
      A. As temperatures rise, much harm will occur.
         1. Farm land will become deserts as temperatures increase. This will lead to food shortages and mass starvation.
         2. As oceans water levels rise, salt water will back up into rivers and destroy fresh water supplies. The lack of water will cause great problems.
            a. Currently 1.2 billion people do not have access to clean water. That number will

increase with global warming, causing
more deaths.

    b. Currently 2 billion people do not have
adequate sanitation causing many people to fall ill. The number of ill people will
increase.

    c. Children are most likely to be the victims
associated with inadequate clean water
supplies.

  3. As farm land and fresh water decreases, more
conflicts over resources will cause war.

  4. Entire countries and islands will disappear
under rising sea water levels affecting over
100 million people.

B. Changes in climate zones will increase diseases
caused by insects.

II. There are many causes of the problem.

  A. Increased usage of fossil fuels is the main cause
of global warming.

    1. Use of inefficient transportation modes like
private automobiles adds to the problem.

    2. Most electricity comes from burning fossil
fuels.

  B. International treaties aren't working.

    1. The United States has not signed the Kyoto
Accords.

2. The European Union ignores the Kyoto Accords.
3. Developing countries do not have to follow the Kyoto Accords.
4. The World Trade Organization encourages growth policies that do not reduce global warming.

III. It will take all of us to reduce global warming.
   A. Society needs to take action.
      1. Green technology needs to be expanded in transportation and energy.
      2. Conservation of fossil fuels requires world-wide policies.
      3. New international treaties with strong initiatives need to be created.
   B. Individuals need to take action.
      1. Conservation begins at home for all of us.
         a. Take public transportation.
         b. Buy energy efficient appliances/autos.
         c. Shut off lights and appliances when not in use.
      2. Activism is for everyone.
         a. Join environmental protection groups.
         b. Start conservation/recycling in your community/campus.
         c. Speak up for the environment.

5. **Summary and Conclusion**: Today we have learned that life on earth is in for a tough future. We now know that global warming will destroy the lives of many and change the way we all live. We have learned that fossil fuel usage and lack of strong government actions is increasing the problem. Finally, we must commit our societies and ourselves to action to reduce global warming before it is too late.

Glossary of Debate Terms

ad hominem attack
Attack on the debater, not the argument.

Affirmative
In some debate formats, the side or team in a debate that support the motion.

analogy
Association between two things based on their similarity; used to support an argument.

analysis
Process of investigating and assessing arguments and refutation.

analysis debate
Debate that asks what the world is like, rather than what should be done about it.

appeal to authority
Fallacy that occurs when a debater takes the status of the person holding an opinion to prove a conclusion.

appeal to the people
Fallacy that occurs when a debater relies on the popularity of an idea as justification for that idea.

argument
Claim supported by reasoning and evidence.

assert
Make a claim.

assertion
A claim.

audience
The people listening to a debate.

ballot
Formal record of results.

begging the question
Fallacy that occurs when a debater introduces evidence that is the same as the claim.

benefits
Positives that a proposition will bring.

body
Arguments and refutation in a speech.

brainstorming
Process of listing as many ideas on a topic as you can think of.

break rounds
At a tournament, the knockout rounds that follow the preliminary rounds.

brief
Written, shortened version of an argument prepared in advance of a debate for quick reference.

burden
Something a team must do to fulfill their role in the debate.

burden of proof
Requirement to demonstrate that something will happen.

burden of refutation
Requirement to disprove an argument.

burden of rejoinder
Requirement to answer refutation and deepen analysis.

case

The position a team take, and the reasons that they take that position.

case statement

The story of the debate as your team see it.

circular argument

Argument that assumes what it is trying to prove.

claim

An assertion. A debater makes claims and supports them with reasoning and evidence to create arguments.

clash

Areas of direct disagreement in a debate.

coach

Person who teaches you how to debate.

conclusion

1) a short dramatic closing to a speech; 2) the claim made by an argument.

consequences

Outcomes resulting from a course of action.

constructive criticism

Comments, often from a judge, about a debate; intended to motivate and improve.

constructive speech

In some formats, a speech that presents a debater's basic arguments for or against a resolution; new arguments are allowed.

costs

Negative outcomes of a course of action.

criteria

Standards against which arguments can be judged in a debate.

critical thinking

Skill that involves thinking about how you think.

cross-examination

In some debate formats, a period during the debate when a member of one team asks questions of a member of the opposing team.

debate

An organized discussion of a topic, with two sides, judged by a third party.

delivery

The way you perform your speeches.

Deputy Leader of the Opposition

In Worlds Style, the second speaker on the Opposition side.

Deputy Prime Minister

In Worlds Style, the second speaker on the Government side.

EFL

English as a Foreign Language; a category at the World University Debating Championships.

energy

Fuel created by nervousness and used to improve delivery.

ESL

English as a Second Language; a category at many Worlds-style debating tournaments.

ethical

Relating to ethics, morals, or principles.

even if

Rhetorical device for establishing clash across a wide range of positions without making concessions.

evidence

Information used to support arguments.

eye contact

Looking somebody directly in the eye.

fallacy

Argument with unsound reasoning.

feedback

Advice given to debaters by judges to help them improve.

floor speech

Speech given by a member of the audience who has watched the debate.

format

Set of rules that govern the debate.

generalization

Forming a conclusion about everyone in group A based on data about some members of group A.

Government

The side in favor of the motion.

grabber

Short introduction designed to get the attention of the listeners.

grounds

See evidence

grouping

Aggregating a set of arguments and refuting them together.

harm

1) a problem that currently exists that the Government seeks to solve; 2) negative outcomes created by a course of action.

inherency

Attitudes or laws that allow a condition to exist; the cause of the problem.

judge

An observer of a debate with the responsibility for deciding the result.

Karl Popper debate

A format that matches two three-person teams against each other.

Leader of the Opposition
In Worlds Style and NPDA, the first speaker on the Opposition.

Lincoln-Douglas debate
A format with one person per team.

manner
Presentation of a speech, including its style and structure.

matter
Content of a speech, including points of information.

Member of the Government
In Worlds Style, the third speaker on the Government side. In NPDA, the Affirmative speaker who speaks after the Leader of the Opposition.

Member of the Opposition
In Worlds Style, the third speaker on the Opposition side. In NPDA, the Negative speaker who speaks after the Member of the Government.

monotone
Speaking everything with the same pitch.

motion
Topic to be debated.

motivation
Reason behind your delivery style. Body language should be motivated.

narrative
Presenting information by telling a story in your own words.

Negative
In Lincoln-Douglas and Policy debate, the side that rejects the motion.

non sequitur
Argument in which the claim does not follow from the reasoning.

note-taking
Keeping a brief written record to use in your speech.

novice
Beginner debater, with no or little experience of debating.

NPDA
National Parliamentary Debate Association; an American debate format between two teams of two speakers.

Opponent
Term used for teams on the other side, regardless of what side you are debating.

Opposition
Side opposing the motion.

oral adjudication
Spoken feedback given by judges to debaters to help them improve.

organizing
Putting your content together to create a speech.

pause
Period of silence used deliberately by a debater.

perspective taking
Role-playing to identify the best arguments for an issue.

persuasion
Work done to help people believe what you are saying.

persuasive
Able to make people believe what you are saying.

plan
Course of action proposed by the Government.

point
1) an assertion; 2) an argument.

point not well taken

In NPDA, when a team calls for a point of order and the judge decides to allow the argument to stay in the round.

point of information

Brief comment or question put to a speaker on the opposing side to which she must respond directly.

point of order

In NPDA, an interruption in a rebuttal speech to ask the judge to decide whether a new argument has been offered.

point well taken

In NPDA, when a team calls for a point of order and the judge decides not to allow the argument to stay in the round.

policy

Proposition that a body should take action.

policy debate

Format in which two teams of two speakers debate a policy.

post hoc fallacy

Fallacy that occurs when a debater assumes that because one event happened before another, the first must have caused the second.

practicalities

Arguments about whether a plan will work.

preliminary rounds

The beginning rounds in a tournament in which all teams take part.

preparation time or prep

Time allotted to each team for preparation before or during a debate.

preview

Brief outline of your speech.

Prime Minister
In Worlds Style and NPDA, the first speaker on the Government side.

principles
Arguments about whether a plan is morally right.

problem
Issue or harm that you are seeking to address.

proof
Reasoning and evidence that supports a claim.

proposition
1) a course of action or position put forward by the Government; 2) in some debate styles, the Government.

proposition of policy
Recommendation that a certain action be taken.

proposition of value
Statement that tries to prove an opinion.

public speaking
Talking in front of an audience.

reasoning
Logical explanation that supports a claim.

rebut
Explaining what is wrong with an argument.

rebuttal
1) process of explaining what is wrong with arguments; 2) in some formats, special speeches that challenge and defend arguments introduced in constructive speeches.

recent, relevant, and reliable
Three tests for the usefulness of evidence.

red herring
Fallacy by which a debater shifts focus away from the original argument.

refutation

Process of attacking arguments and showing them to be weaker than yours.

refute

Prove something wrong.

rejoinder

Process of answering refutation and deepening analysis.

repeat

Say your opponents' argument again.

replace

Make an argument that is more persuasive than your opponents'.

research

Process of locating and selecting evidence in preparation for debate.

role

Individual or team position in a debate.

rounds

All of the teams are debating at the same time.

shorthand

System of writing using abbreviations and symbols to rapidly record what is being said.

side

Every debate has two sides: one supporting the motion, and one against it.

signposting

Telling listeners what you are going to say in the order you are going to say it.

solvency

How the proposal will solve a problem.

standards

Criteria against which values can be judged.

state your point
In NPDA, what a judge says when a team calls out "point of order."

statistics
Evidence expressed in numbers.

status quo
Current state of affairs.

straw man
Fallacy that occurs when a debater attacks a weakened version of an opponent's argument.

structure
Organization of the content of a speech to aid effective presentation.

style
Language, voice, and body language of a debater.

subjective opinion
Beliefs or attitudes of an individual.

summary
Restatement of the points in a speech and how they further a case.

tautology
Definition in which a term is defined using the same term.

testimonial
Statement in support of a fact or claim.

term
Word or phrase.

This House
In Worlds Style, the conventional way to start the wording of the motion.

topic
Area for discussion or debate.

tournament
Series of debates in which debaters or teams of debaters attempt to win.

vocal variety
Differences in tone, pace, and volume that are part of delivery.

Whip
In Worlds Style, the final speaker on each side.

Worlds Style
Format of debate used at the World University Debating Championships.

World University Debating Championships
Annual tournament that determines the World Champions of debate among university students.